This Text Book is useful for Sir Parashurambhau College of Arts, Science and Commerce, Pune. (Autonomous)

Business Administration

S.Y.Bcom. (Sem. - IV) (Course Code : BA24126)

Dr. Sunil S. Shete

(M.Com., B.Ed., G. D. C. & A., M. Phil., Ph.D.)

Joint Director, Higher Education, Pune.

Dr. M. G. Mulla

(M.Com., M.M.S., M.Phil., P.G.D.I.B. D.T.L. DLL & LW G.D.C&A., Ph.D.)

MCE Society Abeda Inamdar Senior College of Arts, Science and Commerce, Pune.

Dr. Nandini Deshpande

(M.Com., M.Phil., M.B.A. (H.R.), D.I.M., Ph.D.)

Sinhgad College Arts and Commerce, Narhe, Pune.

2023

Price. 110/-

SUCCESS PUBLICATIONS

Published by

Dr. Rajesh M. Patne

Success Publications

Radha Krishna Apartment, 535, Shaniwar Peth,

Appa Balwant Chowk, Opp. Prabhat Talkies, Pune - 411 030.

Ph. 24434662 Mobile : 9325315464.

Printed at

Success Publications

S.No. 30/27, Laxmi Industrial Estate,

Near Prabhat News Paper, Dhayari, Pune-41.

Edition

2023

Edited By

Miss. Rajashree Patne

Typesetting, Layout

Miss. Varsha Lokhande

Cover Designing

Miss. Varsha Lokhande

ISBN NO. - 978-81-962519-7-0

Preface

It is a matter of great pleasure for us to present this book to our esteemed readers. This book has been designed as standard text on 'Business Administration ' for S.Y.Bcom (Sem. - IV)

This book comprehensively covers the entire syllabus of SYBCOM Course of Sir Parashurambhau College (Autonomous), Pune effective from June 2020 onwards. It has been written to meet the requirements of students of S.Y.Bcom. Some of the special features of the book are as follows :

1. *Full coverage of the revised syllabus of S.Y.Bcom.*
2. *Chapter outline at the beginning of each chapter to give a bird's eye view of the topics covered in the chapter.*
3. *Pointwise explanation of each topic in the chapter.*
4. *Topics are logically arranged in numbered paragraphs exactly according to the modified syllabus.*
5. *Proposed questions at the end of each chapter.*
6. *Extensive use of diagrams, tables and various forms to give visual view of key concepts and techniques.*
7. *Conversational, lucid and simple language.*

Every effort has been made to provide the readers with most up-to-date and authentic material on the subject.

We are very grateful to our publisher Mrs. and Mr. Rajesh Patne who have rendered all possible assistance in bringing out this book. We wish to acknowledge our deep gratitude to staff who have assisted and helped us in preparing this book. We will consider our efforts amply rewarded in case the book proves useful to the students and teachers of the subject.

Suggestions of readers are welcome and shall be acknowledged with gratitude.

With best wishes,

By Authors

Syllabus

S. Y.B.Com (Sem. - IV)

Business Administration (Paper Code : BA24126)

Unit	Contents	Lectures
1	**Legal Aspects (Recent Trends) :**	12
	1.1 Compliance of Legal Requirements in Promoting Business Unit,	
	1.2 Licensing, Registration	
	1.3 Filing Returns and Other Documents	
2	**Productivity :**	12
	2.1 Meaning	
	2.2 Importance & Measurements of Productivity	
	2.3 Factors Affecting Productivity	
	2.4 Role of National Productivity Council	
	2.5 Product Quality Control	
3	**Business Liasoning :**	12
	3.1 Interface between Business and Government	
	3.2 Society ,and Natural Environment; etc	
	3.3 Business Strategy: Meaning and Importance and Steps in Developing Strategies	
4	**Business Alliances (Growth Strategies):**	12
	4.1 Business Alliance - Meaning and Definition	
	4.2 Growth Strategies - Expansion	
	4.3 Integration and Diversification	
	4.4 Mergers & Acquisition	
	4.5 Franchising - Concept and Characteristics	
	4.6 Public Private Partnership - Meaning and Features	
	Total	**48**

INDEX

S. Y.B.Com (Sem. - IV)

Business Administration (Paper Code : BA24126)

Unit	Contents	Page No.
1	**Legal Aspects (Recent Trends)**	1.1 to 1.19
	▶ 1.1 Compliance of Legal Requirements in Promoting Business Unit ▶ 1.2 Licensing ▶ 1.3 Registration ▶ 1.4 Filing Returns and other Documents	
2	**Productivity**	2.1 to 2.17
	▶ 2.1 Productivity ▶ 2.2 National Productivity Council ▶ 2.3 Product Quality Control	
3	**Business Liasoning**	3.1 to 3.20
	▶ 3.1 Interface between Business and Government, Society and Natural Environment ▶ 3.2 Business Strategy	
4	**Business Alliance (Growth Strategies)**	4.1 to 4.27
	▶ 4.1 Businesss Alliance ▶ 4.2 Growth Strategies - Expansion ▶ 4.3 Integration and Diversification ▶ 4.4 Mergers and Acquisition ▶ 4.5 Franchising ▶ 4.6 Outsourcing ▶ 4.7 Public Private Partnership	

Legal Aspects (Recent Trends)

UNIT 1

- 1.1 Compliance of Legal Requirements in Promoting Business Unit
- 1.2 Licensing
- 1.3 Registration
- 1.4 Filing Returns and other Documents

Introduction :

The Government's liberalisation and economic reforms programme aims at rapid and substantial economic growth, and integration with the global economy in a harmonized manner. The industrial policy reforms have reduced the industrial licensing requirements, removed restrictions on investment and expansion, and facilitated easy access to foreign technology and foreign direct investment. To promote any business unit number of legal requirement are to be complied with. There are different types of business ownership forms. They are covered under various laws in India. To start business some legal formalities, such as licenses, registration and other related documents are to be completed. The different laws contain different important legal provisions governing the promotion and establishment of unit. These provisions and formalities are discussed in this chapter.

1.1 Compliance of Legal Requirements in Promoting Business Unit :

A business unit is established for earning profit by producing and distributing goods and services. There are various forms of business organisation based on nature and size of business, sole trading, partnership, Co-operative societies, public and private companies are the main forms of business unit. Common legal formalities for any business unit are as follows:

1.1.1 Legal Requirements for Promoting a Business Unit :

Starting a business is a daunting task. It requires many technicalities and procedures, which need to be followed so that the business may run with ease and make maximum profits. Firstly, a business which just steps into the industry needs to have a firm foundation.

Unfortunately, many businesses start to flounder just because of the humongous amount of business formalities preceding and superseding the start of a business.

At its core, a good business structure requires an astute business model and a prudent legal foundation. The chosen legal system should ideally enable one's business to grow with minimal intervention. For this, the new business needs to know which legal system will cater to the needs of their particular business model. Therefore, it is very important to know the practical aspect of how to set-up and select one's ' business to ensure success in the industry.

1) Incorporation of a Business Entity :

The first step in starting a business is to decide on the format of entity for conducting the business. This is an important decision: the right type of business entity will support your business plan and help accelerate your business growth. You may also be able to avoid high tax rates and prevent personal liabilities in case of a loss. A business may be set up in India by way of a proprietorship, One Person Company, Partnership, Limited Liability Company, Private Limited Company and Public Limited Company.

a) Types of business Units :

A business may be set up in India in one of the following formats. Each business format is suited for specific uses and has its advantages and limitations. While it is possible to convert a business from one format to the other, it may involve significant time, effort and expense.

i) Proprietorship :

A proprietorship is a business entity that is owned and managed by a single person, called a proprietor. This is the simplest form of business and is easy to set up. In India, most independent professionals conduct business as proprietorships - examples are doctors, chartered accountants, lawyers and local shops and outlets. Unlike other forms of business, there is no specific procedure prescribed for setting up of a proprietorship. A proprietorship does not have an income tax identity separate from its owner. The existence of a proprietorship is shown by its registrations in its name. Registrations under the Shops and Establishment Act, the Service Tax Act, under the MSME provisions, etcetera are sufficient as proof of existence of the proprietorship.

ii) One Person Company (OPC) :

A One Person Company (OPC) is a recent concept introduced under the Companies Act, 2013. OPC provides a systematic legal framework for an entrepreneur who wishes to launch a venture on his own. OPC has only one shareholder, who should be a citizen of India and resident in India. This shareholder has to nominate another person to become the shareholder of the OPC in case of death or incapacity of the original shareholder. The nominee should also be a citizen of and resident in India. OPCs offer all the advantages of a Company, namely: (a) limited liability, (b) perpetual existence, and (c) independent legal standing. Accordingly, it also is required to comply with the provisions applicable to a Company such as auditing of accounts, filing of annual returns, etcetera. Further, the tax slabs applicable to a Company also apply to OPCs. If the paid up share capital of the OPC exceeds Rupees 50 Lac or the annual turnover of the OPC exceeds Rs. 2 Crore during a year, such OPC is compulsorily required to convert into a private limited company or a public limited company.

iii) Partnership :

A partnership is a business owned jointly by two or more persons who have agreed to share profits of the business. This is among the most common business formats seen in India today. A partnership can have a maximum of 20 partners. The partnership agreement gives the partners complete flexibility to decide on matters such as capital contribution, management of affairs and distribution of profits. Commonly, partnership firms are set up in case of small and mid-sized businesses in which the owners themselves provide specialised services. Examples of partnership firms are legal firms, accounting and auditing firms and engineering firms.

iv) Limited Liability Partnership (LLP) :

An LLP is a legal entity which is a hybrid of a partnership (in terms of its constitution) and a company (in terms of protection from unlimited liability). In terms of liability protection, a partner is liable only to the extent of his agreed upon capital contribution. Further, a partner cannot be held personally liable for independent or unauthorized acts of any other partner. However, such independent or unauthorized acts will bind the LLP itself. The operations of an LLP are managed as per the provisions of the LLP Agreement, which is also called the Partnership Deed

v) Private Limited Company :

A private limited company is a form of business which has its own legal existence separate from that of its owners. It has two attractive features: protection of limited liability to the owners and the ease of transfer of ownership. Unlike other formats, there is a separation of ownership and management of a private limited company. The owners of the company - called as 'shareholders' - do not actively participate in the management of the business. The business decisions are taken by a team of people called as 'Directors', who are elected by the shareholders from time to time.

vi) Public Limited Company :

A public limited company is a form of business which is suited to mature businesses. In addition to the advantages of a private limited company, a public limited company permits its shareholders to freely transfer their shares. This form of business is highly regulated, and there are several restrictions which a public limited company has to follow.

b) Incorporation of a Company :

Company is established through legal procedure and has a separate legal entity from its owners. Legal procedure of establishment a company is termed as incorporation. For this purpose, registration of company has to be made with the Registrar of companies. An entrepreneur is required to submit an application for registration following documents:

i) Application form duly filled in and signed by an authorized person.

ii) **Memorandum of Association :**

The Memorandum of Association is the charter of the company. This includes its objectives, its name, the address of its registered office, the capital which the company is authorised to raise, the nature of liability of members as well as the names, addresses and agreement of people who agree to form a company.

iii) **Articles of Association :**

The other important document is the articles of association which contains the rules and regulations relating to the internal management of the company. However, it is not necessary for a public company limited by shares to file the articles of association. If such public company does not file Articles of Association, it is deemed to have adopted 'Table A' of schedule I of the Act.

iv) **Written Consent of the Directors :**

Written consent of the directors who are agreed to act in that capacity, duly signed by each director, along with a written undertaking by them to take the necessary qualification shares, if any, as provided in the articles.

v) A copy of agreement with any individual for appointment as a managing director, or a whole-time director or manager.

vi) A statutory declaration stating that all the legal requirements of the Act precedent to incorporation have been complied.

vii) A letter of intent under Industries (Development and Regulation) Act, 1951, if the company s business comes with the purview of this Act.

viii) Address of registered office of the company. However a company may file registered address within 30 days of its registration.

ix) At the time of registration, the prescribed registration fees and filing fee for each document filed for registration are to be paid to the Registrar's office. After receiving these documents, Registrar scrutinise these documents and if he is satisfied that all the documents are in order, he shall enter the name of the company in the register of companies and issue a certificate of incorporation.

c) Capital Subscription :

Next step in the registration of a company is to raise capital for the proposed company. Company obtains the necessary capital by selling shares to the public. Following procedure is adopted for this purpose:

i) Permission of public issue from 'The Securities and Exchange Board of India.

ii) Agreements with the underwriters, brokers and share issue managers.

iii) Filing a copy of prospectus with the Registrar.

iv) Invite the public to purchase the shares of the company by putting the prospectus in circulation.

v) Receiving applications for shares through the company's banker.

vi) Formal resolution of allotment, if the subscribed capital is at least equal to minimum subscription of 90% of capital issue.

vii) In case, minimum subscription is not received, the entire amount with application would have to be refunded at the end of 120 days from the circulation of prospectus.

viii) Issue of allotment letters and share certificates.

ix) In case a company having a share capital, but not issuing a 'prospectus', filing a 'Statement in lieu of Prospectus' with the Registrar at least three days before the first allotment resolution.

d) Commencement of Business :

A public company cannot commence business immediately after incorporation unless it has obtained a certificate of commencement of business from the Registrar. Following documents have to be filed for this purpose :

i) Shares payable in cash have been allotted to the extent of the minimum subscription;

ii) Every director has paid in cash the application and allotment money on the shares taken by him;

iii) No money is liable to be refundable to the applicants for failure to apply or obtain permission for the shares or debentures to be dealt in on any recognised stock exchange. A statutory declaration duly verified by one of tho directors or the secretary in the proscribed form that the above conditions have been complied with has been filed with the Registrar.

The Registrar will scrutinize those documents and if he is satisfied, he shall issue a "certificate of commencement of Business, This certificate is conclusive evidence that the company can commence its business and use its borrowing powers.

2) Discuss, Prepare and Sign the Founder's Contract :

Often, founders start off the venture on an oral understanding of various crucial issues, without putting matters down on paper. This is mainly due to lack of knowledge, disinclination for paperwork or just mutual awkwardness to discuss the issue.

However, as the business grows and prospers uncertainties about important matters could be the cause of disagreements. Even if co-founders are best friends from school, family members or trusted past-business associates, they may not be using the same vocabulary when it comes to discussing the setting up of the new venture. Therefore, it is necessary to have a very clear agreement among the founders / partners about the investments and the distribution of profits.

Some of the issues that need to be discussed and agreed upon among the founding team are:

a) Dealing with shares of a founder who leaves the business.
b) The decision making system of the business.
c) The ownership structure of the business.
d) The roles and responsibilities of the founders.
e) The modalities of addition of a new partner in the future.
f) Protection of founders who do not have a majority stake in the business.

It is advisable for each member of the founding team to identify and talk about the various issues that need to be recorded in writing. The impact of future plans of the company - such as infusion of venture capital – should be discussed. On the basis of these discussions, a legal agreement should be drawn up in simple terms, capturing the key details. The founders' agreement should be read and understood by each founder to his or her satisfaction, before signing. An original set of this agreement should be retained by, with each partner, and the agreed upon provisions should ideally be included in the Articles of Association of the venture.

3) **Obtain the Required Registrations and Licenses :**

A business is required to be registered with various government authorities, depending on its nature and activities of the business. In most cases, your business will be required to file statements with the government from time to time. The following are the various registrations and licenses which may be required by business to operate a business in India:

a) Import Export Code (IEC) if the business involves import or export.
b) Employees' Provident Fund Organization.
c) Value-Added Tax (VAT) if the business involves sale of goods.
d) Shop and Establishment License for physical premises.
e) Permanent Account Number (PAN) for income tax.
f) Taxation Account Number (TAN) for withholding of tax.
g) Service Tax Number if your business involves providing services.
h) Professional Tax Registration.
i) Employees' Insurance (ESIC).

Further, depending on the industry in which it operates, the business may be required to obtain specific licenses, such as a FSSAI license for food manufacturers, storage, transporters, distributors, etc.

4) Trademark Brands :

As business grows, so does its goodwill. It is therefore necessary for to protect business trade name, logo, tag line, and key phrases from misuse. Trademark is a combination of words and pictures which is registered with the government as belonging to business. Trademark gives protection against misappropriation of value that creates in business through branding and advertising. Under the process of the existing law, registering a trademark typically takes about two to three years; however, business can start using the term "TM" next to its name from the date on which the application for the same is filed. It is advisable to file for business trademark at an early stage, before start business branding activities.

5) Organisation of Accounting and Taxation Systems :

A well-designed accounting system is among the most important parts of business. Without it, business would not be able to keep a track of the various transactions conducted by persons - the assets it owns, to whom it owes money and amounts receivable from its customers.

A strong accounting system could be the dashboard of company's finances, helps to understand the answers to various questions such as:

a) How could scale up business operations and how should finance this growth?

b) In what areas could course corrections be made to ensure a healthier financial position?

c) Are things going as per business plan or are there any course corrections that need to make?

d) What discounts and credit periods can afford to offer to customers?

e) How could prepare and analyses meaningful 'what-if' scenarios for taking strategic and tactical decisions?

Failure to have a well-designed and robust accountancy function robs of the opportunity to review rich data and draw meaningful inferences for decision making.

6) Create Business Policies :

Building an industry-leading venture needs support of stakeholders - clients, vendors and employees. Having coherent documented systems allows the organisation to present a clear framework of relationships. Clients appreciate the missions, values and functioning methodology of the business. Vendors are aware of the procurement and quality policies. Employees know the venture's expectations and operational framework. Well-structured policies facilitate the evolution of the best principles of corporate governance at the venture. Some of the policies that are relevant for a business to develop are as under.

Operational Policies :

a) Marketing Policy (advertising guidelines, commission structure, client satisfaction parameters)

b) Website Terms and Conditions

c) Human Resource Separation Policy (retirement, resignation, termination, notice, handover, full and final, etc.)

d) IT Policy (level of access, restricted sites, backups, checkups, etc.)

e) Use of Official Assets Policy (use of company's laptops, vehicles, guesthouses, etc.)

f) Human Resource Policy (Recruitment, training, travel, reporting, attendance, reimbursement, leave, disciplinary)

g) Rewards Policy (appraisals, increments, promotions, benefits, etc.)

h) Code of Conduct (corporate culture, sexual harassment, conflict of interest, whistle-blower, etc.)

i) Sales Policy (invoicing, discounts, payments, product return, interest on delayed payments, after-sales, etc.)

7) Small Unit Registration Certificate :

The entrepreneur of a small scale unit should seek registration of his selected project unit with the Directorate of industries. This will make the entrepreneur and his unit eligible for availing Government assistance. A unit is normally registered provisionally first and accorded permanent registration later.

1.1.2 Various Acts Related to Promotion and Establishment of a Business Unit :

The provisions laid down by the following acts are governing the promotion and establishment of the unit:

1) Factory Act, 1948 :

This act governs the small industries in which there are more than 10 workers. Indian standard Institutes rules have to be followed by the new industries According to this Act. Drug Control Act controls the pharmaceuticals companies.

2) MRTP / FEMA :

Monopolies Restricted Trade Practices and Foreign Exchange Regulation Act, these two acts govern the licensing policy of the industries according to the new industrial policy of 1991. Many industries are exempted from the licensing system. These are the two main Acts providing major legal provisions in promoting a business unit.

3) Bombay Shops and Establishment Act, 1948 :

This act clears the legal provisions regarding registration and establishment of the business. The industries started in corporation area have to register their business according to the act.

Thus in promoting the business the provisions are mainly regarding registration and licensing of the unit. It depends upon the organisation that which acts will govern the unit e.g. Co-operative Societies are governed by the Co-operative Societies Act of 1912, Partnership Companies are governed by Partnership Act of 1932. Sole Trading is governed by local authorities such as corporation, Gram Panchayat. Joint stock companies are governed by Indian Companies Act of 1956.

4) **In Establishing the Unit, following Acts are Governing the Business :**

In establishment of the unit, capital rising especially in case of public limited company is considered. To follow the rules regarding employees welfare Acts, Pollution Acts, Acts regarding Taxes have the main role in providing the legal provisions regarding establishment the unit.

a) **Companies Act of 2013 :**

The Act has provided the legal consideration in raising the share capital. Filing the returns, submitting the various documents with the Registrar of companies are the main legal provisions made by this Act. Company can raise the share capital by following the rules and regulations of the Act and SEBI.

b) **Other Acts Useful in Establishing the Business Unit :**

The Act such as, Indian Trade Union Act, 1926, Industrial Disputes Act of 1946, Consumer rights Act, Employees welfare Act, Sale tax Act, 1926, Income Tax Act, 1926, Contract Act, Drug Control Act, 1926, Patent Act, Bonus Act

▶ 1.2 Licensing :

A license is a written permission from the government to an industrial unit to manufacture goods specified in the permission letter. A license to run an industry also specifies such particulars as the location, details regarding product, capacity of the unit etc. An Industrial license is an important instrument of state policy. The prime objective of the licensing system is to give effect to the industrial policy of the Government It helps in achieving inter sectoral balance between public sector, organised private sector and small scale sector. Three fold classifications of industries are done for licensing i.e. Core sector, joint sector and middle sector. Different types of industries require different type of licenses e.g. food products industry requires FPO license (Food Products Organisation).

1.2.1 Legislative Framework for Licensing :

Three different acts are passed for providing a legal framework for licensing systems. Industries Development and Regulation Act, 1951, Monopolies and Restrictive Trade Practices Act (MRTP), 1969, Foreign Exchange Regulation Act, 1973.

1) **Working of the Act :**

At present, 79 important industries excluding plantation industries are covered by the Act. The Government has wide powers of controlling and regulating private enterprises in the country. It can make periodical investigation of the working of the industries covered by the act.

2) Registration and Licensing of Undertakings :

After the commencement of the Act, all existing undertakings included under the Act are supposed to be registered with the Government. New undertaking Covered by the Act is required to obtain a license from the Government before establishing. The same applies to any substantial additions that may be made to existing licensed undertaking licensing of new undertaking enables the Government to regulate such important aspect of private enterprise as size, location, manufacturing programme etc. in national interest.

3) Exemption Limit for Licensing :

Industrial concerns with an investment of less than Rs. 1 crore do not require a license. Industrial units having fixed assets of less than Rs. 5 crore need not obtain any license under the Industries Act.

1.2.2 Business License in India :

Once upon a time, India was known as the land of the 'license raj'. However, after reforms in 1991, setting up businesses in India, by and large, has become less complex and cumbersome compared to the pre-1991 era, according to observers. An individual who wishes to run a business not only has to research and finalize his business plan, funding and servicing/product model but also comply with various regulations and obtain the required licenses in India.

Business licenses are primarily issued by the government to allow individuals to run businesses. It is important to note that a license which has to be issued will be based on the business requirements of a company after its registration or incorporation. However, there are various other factors which may also determine the type of license which has to be issued such as the type of business ownership, business location and number of employees among others. There are various types of business license issued in India as listed below:

1) Shops and Establishment License :

A shop has to mandatory register itself under the Shops and Establishment Act under 30 days of commencement of operations. In many cases, there are different laws for different states in the country such as Bombay Shops and Establishments Act 1948, Karnataka Shops and Establishments Act 1961 and Delhi Shops and Establishments Act, 1954 among others. The businesses which come under the ambit of the Shops and Establishments Act are as follows:

a) A movie theater or any public amusement area.

b) Trading or insurance companies.

c) Restaurant, cafe, eating joint or hotels.

d) Administrative service which employs individuals for office work.

The Shops and Establishment Act covers various pertinent aspects such as working hours (day and week), maintenance of records, opening and closing hours, overtime, national holidays, and religious holidays, employment of women, maternity leave, and termination of service, casual leave and display of notices among others.

2) TAN :

Tax Deduction and Collection Account Number or TAN is a 10-digit alphanumeric number which has to be quoted by individuals who have to collect or deduct tax on payments made by them on behalf of the income tax department. For instance individuals who pay salaries and rent should ensure that tax is deducted at source and duly paid to the income tax department. In other words, TAN has to be mandatorily quoted in TCS/TDS returns (not excepting e-TDS returns) and TCS/TDS payment challan among others. As per Section 203A of the Income Tax Act 1961, an assessee who is liable to deduct tax deducted at source has to mandatorily quote his TAN in any TDS related communication with the income tax department. In case TAN is not quoted by an assessee, Rs.10, 000 will be levied as penalty on him. Furthermore, banks will refuse to accept TDS returns if TAN is not quoted.

3) Service Tax Registration :

Service tax is an indirect tax which is levied on certain services as specified by the Government of India under the Finance Act, 1994. A service provider pays service tax to the government. A service provider can collect the service tax from the consumer of service as well in some cases as listed below:

a) Services provided by Foreign Service providers.

b) Services provided by a transport agency.

c) Services provided by mutual fund distributors.

It is important to note that service tax registration should be obtained by any individual who offers a taxable service above Rs. 9 lakhs in a financial year. Also, if a service provider does not obtain service tax registration, he will attract a penalty under section 77 of the Finance Act, 1994. However, small scale service providers who offer taxable services under Rs. 10 lakhs in a financial year are exempt from paying service tax. Service tax should be deposited in select banks on a quarterly (partnership or proprietary firms) and monthly basis (companies and societies).

4) VAT Registration :

VAT is a multi-point tax levied on value addition and therefore, collected at various stages of a sale with a provision for input tax credit. In other words, if VAT is paid on purchases, the amount can be appropriated against VAT on sales. Consequently, the remaining amount is deposited with the state government since VAT is a state-based tax. Each state government has its own specific rules pertaining to VAT depending on the type of goods sold or manufactured. Traders should obtain VAT registration, if they register sales above Rs. 5 lakhs (or Rs. 10 lakhs in some cases) p.a. VAT/CST/TIN utilize the same 11-digit number. VAT is not applicable on goods which are exported from India. Payments related to VAT should be made in select banks only on a quarterly (partnership firms and LLPs) and monthly basis (companies). It is important to note that VAT is borne by consumers.

5) **Professional Tax :**

Professional tax is a tax levied by a state government. Any company which is engaged in any business or an individual engaged in any profession should register and pay professional tax. There are fixed professional tax rates for employers regardless of their declared revenues. Likewise, there are fixed professional tax rates for employees on the basis of income slabs. Professional tax has to be filed on a monthly or quarterly basis.

6) **Central Excise License :**

Central excise duty is an indirect tax which is levied as per Central Excise Act, 1944 on goods manufactured in India. All manufacturers should therefore, obtain central excise registration. A central excise number is a 15-digit number with the first 10 digits of PAN number; the next two digits indicate applicant's status while the last three digits indicate the number of premises. In case a manufacturer does not obtain the central excise registration, he will attract a penalty of Rs. 10,000 or 7 years of imprisonment.

7) **Importer –Exporter Code :**

The Importer Exporter Code (IEC) code is a 10-digit code which is issued by the Ministry of Commerce to individuals and Indian companies for conducting international trade. The importer exporter code has lifetime validity. It is important to note that only one importer exporter code can be obtained on one PAN.

8) **PAN :**

PAN or Permanent Account Number (PAN) is a 10-digit alphanumeric number issued by the income tax department. PAN has to be mandatorily quoted in any document related to financial transactions. In other words, PAN of sellers and buyers should be quoted in the purchase or sale documents of any type of services or goods. All types of businesses, therefore, need to have PAN cards.

1.2.3 Requirement of Licensing for Incorporation :

It is not the firm alone which is benefitted by registration but the parties dealing with the firm are also benefitted. The requirement of incorporation is explained below:

1) **Requires for Corporate personality :**

The primary requirement, from which many other advantages flow, is that the company acquires corporate (or separate, or legal) personality. This means that the company is regarded by the law as a person. Whereas humans are classed as natural persons, the company is a legal person and can therefore do many things that humans can.

2) **Required to the Firm :**
Firm gets the right of filing a case against external parties in the court

3) **Required to the Partners :**
The partners can file a case against one another in case of a conflict. They can also seek the protection of court in defense of their rights against the firm and the outside panics.

4) **Required to Incoming Partner :**
The incoming partner of a registered firm is capable of pleading for his rights, while in case of non-registration of firm he has to depend on the honesty of other partners.

▶ 1.3 Registration :

Business includes every form of trade, commerce, craftsmanship, calling, profession or other activity carried on for the purposes of gain, but does not include any office or employment or any charitable undertaking or any occupation specified in the schedule under the provisions of the Business Registration Act 1956 (ROBA 1956).

1.3.1 Registration Procedure :

Business registration procedure is as follows:

1) Business may be registered using personal name or using a trade name:

a) The business name using personal name as stated in the identity card is not required to apply for business name.
Example: Ruslan bin Mohamed, Siow Ah Thai or, Ramasamy a/l Mutusamy

b) Trade Name is the name of the proposed business and must obtain prior approval from the Registrar of Business.
Example: Kedai Dobi Mewah, Lucky Star Catering or, ABS Unggul Enterprise.

2) Complete the Business Registration Form with the following information :

a) Business name
b) Commencement date of business
c) Principal place of business
d) The address of the branch of business (if any)
e) Information of owner and partners
f) Type of business carried out
g) Provide a copy of the Partnership Agreement (if any)

3) Every business owner and partner must sign the completed Form.

4) Documents to be attached are as follows :

a) Photocopy of owner and/ or partner's identity card;

b) Permit, licence or Supporting letter for the type of business e.g Nurseries (Department of Social Welfare), Kindergarten, Tuition Centres, Schools/College (Ministry/ Department of Education); and

c) Approval or Supporting Letter from relevant agency if required by the Registrar of Business.

1.3.2 Requirement :

Requirement for registration is as follows :

1) Owner must be an Indian Citizen or Permanent Resident of India.
2) Owner must be aged between 18 years and above.
3) Register the business not later than thirty (30) days from the date of commencement of business.
4) The nature of the registered business should not contravene any laws or likely to be used for unlawful purposes or any purpose prejudicial to or incompatible with the security of the Federation, public order or morality.

1.3.3 General Guide :

1) A new business registration may valid for a period of one (1) year and does not exceed five (5) years on each registration.
2) Business Registration Certificate can be obtained within one (1) hour from the time payment is made.
3) Even though businesses have been registered with SSM, business owners are responsible to obtain licenses, permits or approval letters from other relevant authorities in order to operate their businesses.

1.3.4 Documents Required for Application of Registration :

The following documents are to be enclosed with the application of registration :

1) The ground plan of the premises of the factory.
2) The brief information about the manufacturing process of his goods or products.
3) In case of partnership, copy of Partnership Deed, Memorandum of Association, Article of Association.
4) In case of Company, Memorandum of Association, copy of board's resolution for authorizing to sign and submit excise documents.
5) The detail of the Pan, residential address of the partners or directors.
6) Power of attorney for signing excise document.
7) Certified copy of incorporation certificate to commence business.
8) Copy of Income Tax PAN.
9) Copy of the factory license or shop establishment certificate, if any.
10) If the premises are owned by the occupant himself/herself then property tax receipt is to be submitted. If it is rented, rent receipt should be enclosed with the application.

11) List of plant and machinery.
12) Details of input with tariff heading and sub-heading.
13) Certified copy of the Sales Tax Registration Certificate.

▶ 1.4 Filing Returns and Other Documents :

A business tax return is basically an income tax return. The return is a statement of income and expenditure of the business. Also, any tax to be paid on the profits made by you is declared in this return. The return also contains details of the assets and liabilities held by the business. Items like fixed assets, debtors and creditors of business, loans taken and loans were given are declared here. Following returns and documents are to be filed with the Registrar:

1) **The Memorandum of Association :**
   It is a documents laying down objects, powers, constitutions and signed by 2 for Pvt. Companies and 7 for public company.
2) **Articles of Association :**
   It is a document which describes all internal rules and regulations and signed by the subscribers to the memorandum.
3) **Notice of Head Office :**
   It is the notice of the address at which the registered office of the company will be situated.
4) **Statutory Declaration :**
   It is a declaration of compliance of legal conditions precedent to incorporation.
5) **Written Consent :**
   Written consent of all directors and their contract for the purchase of qualification shares. These last two documents relating to first directors need not be filed by private companies. On receiving these documents, Registrar of companies issues a formal Incorporation Certificate.
6) **Return of Directors :**
   If a company is to be managed by a managing director it has to fulfill two conditions.

a) Central Government's approval for his appointment.

b) A copy of the return of directors, managers etc. Return of allotment has also to be filed with the registrar within 30 days of allotment.

❋❋❋❋

Objective Type Questions

Q. I. Multiple Choice Questions :

1) **Legal relationship between the middleman and the businessperson is governed by ------------.**
   a) law of business
   b) law of Surety
   c) law of agency
   d) None of the above
2) **Certification mark can be registered in ------------.**
   a) Trademark Registry
   b) Certification Board
   c) Quality Control Board
   d) MHRD
3) **Collective Mark is registered by ------------.**
   a) Partnership firm
   b) Association of person
   c) Individual
   d) Company
4) **Application for approval of name of a company is to be made to ------------.**
   a) SEBI
   b) Registrar of Companies
   c) Government of India
   d) Government of the State in which Company is to be registered
5) **A proposed name of Company is considered undesirable if ------------.**
   a) It is identical with the name of an existing company
   b) It resembles closely with the name of an existing company
   c) It is an emblem of Government of India, United Nations etc.
   d) In case of any of the above
6) **Who can register Geographical Indication?**
   a) Individual
   b) Company
   c) Producers
   d) All of these
7) **A breach of contract can be of ------------ breach**
   a) Discharged
   b) Illegal
   c) Void
   d) None of these
8) **Stages in the formation of a public company are in the following order-----**
   a) Promotion, Commencement of Business, Incorporation, Capital Subscription
   b) Incorporation, Capital Subscription. Commencement of Business, Promotion
   c) Promotion, Incorporation, Capital Subscription, Commencement of Business
   d) Capital Subscription, Promotion, Incorporation, Commencement of Business
9) **The application for registration of a company should be presented to the registrar of the state ------------.**
   a) in which the of the company is to be situated
   b) Manufacturing plant b. first branch

c) business office

d) any of the above

10) Number of documents to be submitted, by a public ltd company, to the registrar while applying for incorporation of the company is ------------.

a) 3 b) 2 c) 7 d) 50

11) The address of the registered office of the company must be notified to the registrar within days of registration, if it is not done at the time of incorporation

a) 15 b) 30 c) 60 d) 45

12) Among the following which documents are not mandatory to be submitted to the registrar along with incorporation application by a private company.

a) Address of Registered office & undertaking

b) Undertaking and statement of capital

c) statement of capital & list of directors

d) list of directors and statement of capital

13) When the registered office of a company is changed within a city then it has to be intimated to the registrar within days of such change ------------.

a) 60 b) 45 c) 30 d) 7

14) The following cannot be exploited by assigning or by licensing the rights to others.

a) Patents b) Designs

c) Trademark d) All of the above

15) The agreement that is enforceable by law is known as ------------.

a) Valid agreement b) Void agreement

c) Illegal agreement d) Unenforceable agreement

16) In which of the following modes of entry, does the domestic manufacturer give the right to use intellectual property such as patent and trademark to a manufacturer in a foreign country for a fee ------------.

a) Licensing b) Contract manufacturing

c) Joint venture d) None of these

17) As per section 139(1), a company shall have to file return of income ------------.

a) when its total income exceeds Rs. 2,50,000

b) when its total income exceeds the maximum amount, which is not chargeable to income -tax

c) in all cases irrespective of any income or loss earned by it

d) in all cases irrespective of any income earned by it

18) As per section 139(1), a firm shall have to file return of income ------------.

a) when its total income exceeds Rs. 2,50,000

b) when its total income exceeds the maximum amount, which is not chargeable to income

c) in all cases, irrespective of any income or loss made by it

d) in all cases irrespective of any income earned by it

19) As per section 139(1), an individual other than an individual of age of 60 years or more shall have to file return of income if ------------.

a) his total income before allowing deduction u/s 80C to 8OU exceeds Rs. 2,50,000

b) his total income before allowing deduction u/s 80C to 80U exceeds Rs. 3,00,000

c) his total income exceeds Rs. 2,00,000

d) his total income before claiming exemption u/s 10(35) and before allowing deduction U/S 80C to 80U exceeds Rs. 2,50,000

20) E-filing of return in case of an office of the Government/company and a firm whose accounts are liable to be audited is ------------.

a) mandatory

b) optional

c) mandatory when its income exceeds Rs. `5,00,000

d) mandatory when its income exceeds Rs. 10,00,000

21) The filing of return of loss in case of a person other than a company or firm is ------------.

a) mandatory

b) not mandatory

c) mandatory if the assessed has to carry forward the loss which are allowed to be carried forward & set off

d) none of the above

22) Person fails to keep, maintain, or retain books of account, documents, etc., as required under section 44AA, penalty shall be leviable ------------.

a) Under section 271A, Rs 10,000 b) Under section 271 A, Rs. 25,000

c) Under section 271B, Rs. 25,000 d) Under section 271B, Rs. 10,000

Ans : 1) c, **2)** a, **3)** b, **4)** b, **5)** d, **6)** d, **7)** a, **8)** c, **9)** c, **10)** c, **11)** b, **12)** a, **13)** c, **14)** c, **15)** a, **16)** a, **17)** c, **18)** c, **19)** b, **20)** a, **21)** c, **22)** b.

Q. II. State the following statement are true or false :

1) Licensing makes the most sense when company manufactures and distributes products and manufacturing facility is operating at capacity.
2) Being a smart, strategic license to a somewhat boring product otherwise can sometime increase the consumer appeal and desire for the product.
3) Being the owner of a valuable and desirable trademark is almost like having a license to steal. People can make great money with very little (or no) effort.
4) If manufacturing facility is operating at less than capacity acquiring a license to make products similar to your own, only with the licensed trademark on it, will fill in the excess production capacity and help lower the overall production costs on other products.
5) When a company is registered with the Registrar of Companies, it obtains the Certificate of Incorporation.
6) If a company is registered on the basis of fictitious names, its incorporation is invalid.
7) If a company is registered on the basis of fictitious names, its incorporation is invalid Options.
8) Registration of a partnership is legally compulsory.
9) Most states require proprietorships to register a business name.
10) The return of income can be filed with the Income-tax Department in electronic mode only.

Ans : **1)** False, **2)** True, **3)** True, **4)** True, **5)** True, **6)** True, **7)** False, **8)** a, **9)** False, **10)** False

Review Questions

Q. 1. Discuss in detail about the Legal requirement for Promoting a Business unit.

Q. 2. Discuss in detail about the Various Acts related to Promotion and Establishment of a Business Unit.

Q. 3. Explain in detail about the Licensing in India.

Q. 4. Explain the Registration Process of Business.

Q. 5. Explain the Filing Returns and Other Documents .

Q. 6. Write Short Notes on Following:

a) Legislative Framework for Licensing.
b) Business License in India.
c) Documents Required for Application of Registration.
d) Registration Procedure.

Productivity

UNIT 2

- 2.1 Productivity
- 2.2 National Productivity Council
- 2.3 Product Quality Control

Introduction :

Productivity is the barometer of industrial development. The study of productivity is important from the point of view of the industries, economy, etc. Productivity is a measure of performance of the economy as a whole. Productivity is a statistical measure. It is a significant tool for analyzing economic matters. Productivity indicates the magnitude of the economic progress and conditions prevailing in the economy. Productivity is a term which indicates individual performance and number of units produced by him in a given time. It is the sign of employee's efficiency. It indicates the 'contribution' made by one worker, one employee to total production. The concept of 'production' relates itself to 'overall performance'. On the other hand the concept of 'productivity' relates itself to individual performance. Since the focus of ergonomics is on people, it is often convenient to think of ergonomic-related problems by the type of body system, which is affected. An ergonomist evaluates the demands of a specific task with reference to the capacity of workers to perfect ill the task over a certain time period. The goal of ergonomics is to fit the task to the individual, not the individual to the task. Practicing good ergonomics achieves increased productivity, improved health and safety of workers, higher job satisfaction and better compliance with government regulations.

2.1 Productivity :

Productivity has now become an everyday watch word. It is crucial to the welfare of industrial firm as well as for the economic progress of the country. High productivity refers to doing the work in a shortest possible time with least expenditure on inputs without sacrificing quality and with minimum wastage of resources. Productivity is an index of efficiency showing the effectiveness of the individual or combined factors used in producing goods or services. Productivity is, thus, the power to produce and indicate the capacity for growth and all material progress of the business. Men, machines, materials, capital, power and services all contribute to productivity and the extent to which each does so may be ascertained by the ratio of output to input. Productivity is an objective concept. As an objective concept it can be measured, ideally against a universal standard. As such, organisations can monitor productivity for strategic reasons such as corporate planning, organization improvement, or comparison to competitors. It can also be used for tactical reasons such as project control or controlling performance to budget.

2.1.1 Meaning :

Productivity means fuller utilisation of resources. It also means elimination of wastes of all types. It also refers to find better, cheaper, quicker and easier ways of doing a job. Productivity is the quantitative relation between what we produce and we use as a resource to produce them, i.e., arithmetic ratio of amount produced (output) to the amount of resources (input). Productivity refers to the efficiency of the production system. It is the concept that guides the management of production system. It is an indicator to how well the factors of production (land, capital, labour and energy) are utilised. Productivity is an economic measure of output per unit of input. Inputs include labor and capital, while output is typically measured in revenues and other GDP components such as business inventories.

2.1.2 Definitions :

Following are the definitions of productivity :

1) **International Labour Organisation :**

   "Productivity is the ratio between the volume of output as measured by production indices and corresponding volume of labour input as measured by employment indices."

2) **P. F. Drucker :**

   "The greatest opportunity for increasing productivity is surely to be founded in knowledge work itself and especially in management".

3) **H. Weihrich :**

   "Productivity as the input - output ratio within a time period with due consideration for quality."

2.1.3 Importance of Productivity :

Increase in production and productivity - both are important for the employer as well as employees in the organisation.

1) **Increase in Production :**

   When the total production increases, supply of goods can be regularly made in the market. Regularity in supply of goods enables to maintain relations with individual and institutional buyers. Customers become confident about the supply of goods at the right time and in right quantity. So, the turnover of the business (sales volume) automatically increases. Increase in production is also a sign of business efficiency, indicator of progress. So status, goodwill of producing concern automatically increases. More and more investors get attracted towards the firm/ industrial unit. Increase in production indirectly benefits the producer. He can claim that whatever investments are made are 'productive' and it is not 'dead investment.'

2) **Increase in Productivity :**

When payments are linked with the 'individual performances', 'piece rate system' is made applicable then increases in productivity increases an income of the employees. The employees get more salaries and wages as reward for the efforts they have made. Increase in productivity is a sign of work performed with utmost devotion. Employee has fully used his capacities and skills in the interest of the company. So the employer feels confident about his colleague employees. This confidence further develops industrial relations. The employer can accept more jobs, orders for supply of goods. Increase in productivity of employee improves his status in the organisation. When honesty and sincerity in work increases, the employer also gives opportunities for progress and promotions in the organisation.

3) **Lower Price :**

Productivity increases the rate of low cost per unit and results in lower price. It helps in retaining whatever competitive advantage that a company may have. It also increases the standard of living since more and more products can be purchased, if product production is more. This way, consumers will benefit from a higher productivity from their business.

4) **Increases Profits For Businesses :**

Productivity increases profits for businesses and will lead to salary increases for laborers. For compassionate capitalists, increased profits mean that they can share more money and blessings with their employees.

5) **Improve Performance :**

Some companies used to say productivity reports are not important as long as their profit level is optimum, but it is wrong. Even though their product levels do not directly represent companies health, but they will help the company executives to improve the performance of the product. It is a way to reward the worthy employees, who excelled in the productivity.

6) **Determines Efficiency of Business :**

Productivity is more important than revenues and profit. This is because profit determines only the end result, whereas productivity determines the efficiency of the business, as well as effectiveness of business processes and policies. Profit does not determine the individual and segment performances.

7) **Measuring Strengths and Weaknesses of an Organisation :**

Another reason why productivity is important for companies is that, it helps them in measuring their strengths and weaknesses alongside the threats and opportunities that the market brings. Once companies determine their weakness, they can work hard and produce expected results.

2.1.4 Measurement of Productivity :

Essentially, productivity measurement is the identification and estimation of the appropriate output and input measures. Productivity measurement is a prerequisite for improving productivity. Measurement plays an important role in management of productivity. It helps to determine if organisation is progressing well. It also provides information on how effectively and efficiently organisation manages its resources. The productivity is measured on account of the following:

A) **Labour Productivity :**

Where most of the work is done by hand labour, measurement of labour productivity is essential. Usually, all factory labour, both direct and indirect should be included. The usual measures of labour productivity are:

1) **In Terms of Hours:**

$$\text{Productivity (i.e. efficiency)} = \frac{\text{Production in Standard hours}}{\text{Possible (or actual) man hours}}$$

$$\text{Lost time Percentage} = \frac{\text{Man hours lost}}{\text{Possible man hours}} \times 100$$

2) **In Terms of Money:**

By any one of these ratios:

$$\frac{\text{Sales value (or cost) of output}}{\text{Number of Workers}}$$

OR

$$\frac{\text{Direct wages}}{\text{Sales value}}$$

OR

$$\frac{\text{Indirect Wages}}{\text{Direct Wages}}$$

OR

$$\frac{\text{Direct wages}}{\text{Number of units}}$$

Productivity of labour can therefore be increased by increasing efficiency of labour, reducing idle time and improving the working conditions of labour and undertaking effective labour welfare schemes as mentioned earlier.

B) Material and Purchase Efficiency :

In case of new product a good design may reduce the wastage and excess usage of material. At the operation stage, higher productivity is achieved by using minimum material with the help of skilled workmanship, adequate machine tools and quality and efficient purchases. An idea of productivity can be obtained from the following ratios:

1) Material Productivity :

Any one of the ratios:

$$\frac{\text{Material Cost}}{\text{No.of units produced}}$$

OR

$$\frac{\text{Direct Material cost}}{\text{Production Cost}}$$

OR

$$\frac{\text{Indirect Material Cost}}{\text{Material Cost}}$$

OR

$$\frac{\text{Ditrect Material Cost}}{\text{Sales}}$$

OR

$$\frac{\text{Direct Material Consumed}}{\text{No. of Employee}}$$

OR

$$\frac{\text{Rejected or Waste or Scrap}}{\text{Total Material Consumed}}$$

2) Purchase Efficiency:

By the following ratios:

$$\frac{\text{Actual Purchase Price}}{\text{Budjeted Purchase Price}}$$

OR

$$\frac{\text{Purchase in Current Period}}{\text{Purchase in Previous Period}}$$

OR

$$\frac{\text{Purchase Return}}{\text{Total Purchase}}$$

OR

$$\frac{\text{Purchase Cost or T.D. earned}}{\text{Total Purchase}}$$

C) Machine Productivity:

In a highly mechanized factory, capacity utilisation of machinery is more important than full utilisation of other factors. Machine productivity is determined by:

1) Machine Utilisation :

$$\text{Machine Utilisation (Productivity)} = \frac{\text{Output in Standard hours}}{\text{Planned (or actual) machine hours}}$$

2) Activity percentage:

$$\text{Activity Percentage} = \frac{\text{Acutal Machines hours}}{\text{Planned Machine hours}} \times 100$$

3) Lost Time Percentage:

$$\text{Lost time Percentage} = \frac{\text{Machine hours lost}}{\text{Planned Machines hours}} \times 100$$

4) Machine Effectiveness:

$$\text{Machine Effectiveness} = \frac{\text{Net Machine running time + setting up time}}{\text{Total working hours of plan group}}$$

5) Output per Machine Hour:

$$\text{Output per machine hour} = \frac{\text{Output}}{\text{Actual machine hours}}$$

D) Productivity of Power and Services:

The effective utilisation of power and other services is essential in every business organisation and the following ratios are useful to calculate the productivity.

$$\frac{\text{Horse power utilisex}}{\text{No. of hours worked}}$$

OR

$$\frac{\text{Maintainance Cost}}{\text{No. of hours worked}}$$

E) Selling Distribution and Administration Productivity :

$$\frac{\text{Selling, Distribution and Administration Costs}}{\text{Total Sales}}$$

OR

$$\frac{\text{Salesman's Salary and Commission etc.}}{\text{Total Sales}}$$

OR

$$\frac{\text{Advertising Cost}}{\text{Total Sales}}$$

2.1.5 Factors affecting Productivity :

The individual performances of all employees in the organisation cannot be uniform. It is all accepted truth. There are limitations for the capacity of every individual. These limitations are in respect of stress and strain that one person bare. Over burdening of employee in the long run have some serious consequences. Following are the factors affecting on productivity:

1) **Technological Factors :**

   Technology refers to the use of mechanical power, automatic machines, efficient integration of plant and machinery, specialisation of work and output, etc. The technology or method of work and productivity are related. The use of motive power or mechanical power increases productivity and accelerates the pace of industrialisation.

   In underdeveloped countries the working conditions are bad, methods are wasteful of time and effort. Valuable machines are kept idle due to the shortage of raw material and lack of repairs. There is lack of proper lighting, ventilation and lay-out. All this adversely affects productivity.

2) **Financial Factors :**

   Finance or capital is very important factor influencing productivity. Capital is required for the introduction of new methods of production or technology. Finance is required for many things like providing facilities to the workers, modernisation of plant and machinery, etc. Research also requires funds. It is observed that the capital abundant countries have high productivity.

3) Natural Factors :

These factors include availability of resources, climate, etc. The Agro-based industries depend upon nature to a greater extent. So, favourable natural conditions improve the productivity. The climatic differences have a significant influence on industrial efficiency and productivity.

4) Sociological Factors :

This factor refers to the social values, customs, traditions, caste system, religion, etc. The Modern Industries expect practical and scientific attitude of the people. They expect the workers to overcome the language, caste and religions barriers. The society should be ready to accept the new changes. The attitude of the investors, workers and employers should be such that they accept new products and innovations. All these help in improving the productivity.

5) Managerial Factors :

Industries require energetic, talented and trained managers. If they have imagination, organisational capacity and ability to take risk then the productivity increases. Traditional management styles or bossism adversely affects productivity.

6) Government Policies :

Government directly and indirectly influences the industrial productivity. Subsidies have favourable impact on the productivity whereas taxes are likely to lower the productivity. It is observed that if the government does not allow industrial combinations then the small units try to improve the productivity in order to remain in the competition. Government's policy regarding investment also influences the productivity.

Thus, productivity gets affected, favourably or unfavourably by all the factors mentioned above. Productivity growth is the result of a large number of technological, political, institutional, psychological and economic variables.

▶ 2.2 National Productivity Council :

The gains of productivity are generally shared by almost all the sections in the society. These include producers, consumers, employees and the nation itself is one of the beneficiaries. The concept of productivity has received the attention of many groups in the society because productivity is closely connected with the welfare of different groups (means the welfare of masses). In countries like India, it has become a subject matter of national importance. The needs of rapidly growing population cannot be satisfied unless productivity on the whole increases. It has assumed greater importance after independence due to competition in national as well as international level and the need for increasing share in export trade.

Having realised the importance of productivity from different viewpoints, the Government of India appointed a committee on Productivity under the Chairmanship of Dr. Vikram

Sarabhai. He visited Japan and studied in detail the working and administration of Productivity Centre of Japan. The committee submitted its report in March 1957. The recommendations of the committee were found to be very useful and the Government decided to establish the National Productivity Council in February 1958.

It (NPC) is registered as an autonomous body under the separate act, known as Societies Registration Act 1860. In March 1958, its first meeting was held with a view to adopt some concrete programmes.

2.2.1 Objectives of National Productivity Council :

Following are the objectives of National Productivity Council :

1) **Promotion of Productivity Awareness :**
   To stimulate and promote productivity awareness by exchanging information relating to productivity.
2) **Provision of Specialist Services :**
   To make provisions for specialist services if local productivity councils register a demand.
3) **Facilitate Exchange of Views :**
   Encourage industrial or manufacturing concerns for inter plant visits to exchange experiences and views.
4) **Undertake Research :**
   To undertake research and development activities to boost productivity.
5) **Arranging Sponsorship :**
   Sponsorship services arrange visits of productivity teams to economically advanced countries to collect important information which is helpful to increase productivity.
6) **Inviting Foreign Exports :**
   Inviting foreign experts for guidance purposes in order to attain the goal of progress of various industrial units and institutions in the country.

   NPC is an autonomous body at the national level and it consists of 75 members which represent various groups in the society such as Central Government, employer's representatives, employees representatives, representatives of Local Productivity Councils, (12 members each), representatives of different technical organisations, national organisations.

2.2.2 Role of National Productivity Council :

National Productivity Council plays its role through the following activities :

1) **Arranging Training Programmes :**
   It arranges training programmes relating to important problems, e.g. economical use of fuel and power. It has organised training programmes on large scale for public sector, private sector undertakings.

2) **Organises Seminars :**
It organises seminars and conferences at regional as well as on national levels which provides 'common stage' to discuss problems relating to industrial sector.

3) **Conducting Productivity Surveys :**
NPC also conducts productivity surveys in different areas of management. This activity was started from 1963; it was to some extent in the form of consultation services. General / specific investigations relating to organisation, management, technical problems of enterprises.

4) **Sponsoring Personnel for Training :**
This council sponsors management and technical personnel for attending training courses in foreign countries. It has sent many deserving persons to U.S.A., U.K, West Germany, Japan, France, etc. technically and economically advanced countries.

5) **Increasing Productivity Awareness :**
It has so far made sincere efforts for increasing productivity awareness or consciousness all over the country. It, therefore, organises publication activity also. It collects and publishes information through various journals. These are monthly, quarterly publications. It publishes manuals, case studies also.

6) **Guiding Productivity Councils :**
It guides and supports the activities of Local Productivity Councils and NPC encourages the establishment of such local councils' help for their development.

7) **Supporting Asian Productivity Councils :**
National Productivity Council supports the activities of Asian Productivity councils. It assists the study teams visiting India in the interest of Indian economy and India's industrial sector.

8) **Nationwide Productivity Movement :**
From 1982 onwards, with the help of the Central Government, it has undertaken nationwide movement on productivity awareness. It continuously stresses the need for increasing productivity.

▶ 2.3 Product Quality Control :

Quality control is related to the control of quality during the manufacturing process. It is an important element in every state of production. In other words, quality control is related to the systematic control on those things which affect the quality of any product.

2.3.1 Meaning :

Quality control involves testing of units and determining if they are within the specifications for the final product. The purpose of the testing is to determine any needs for corrective actions in the manufacturing process. Good quality control helps companies meet consumer demands for better products.

2.3.2 Definitions :

Following are the definitions of product quality control :

1) **Alford and Beatty :**

"Quality control may be defined as that industrial management technique or group of techniques by means of which products of uniform acceptable quality are manufactured."

2) **Sigmand P. Zobel :**

"Quality control means seeing to it that the customer gets what he believes he is buying. It is a cost reduction programme."

2.3.3 Quality Circle :

A quality circle or quality control circle is a group of workers who do the same or similar work, who meet regularly to identify, analyze and solve work-related problems. It consists of minimum three and maximum twelve members in number.

A) Meaning :

Quality circle is related to small groups of workers belonging to the same area or group who voluntarily perform quality control activities and tries to solve the problems related to their workshop. Quality Circles first developed in Japan during the late 1950's and early 1960's. It is related to the Japanese experience. This concept is result of Japanese concern for statistical quality control. It emerges due to the two reasons. Firstly, there was the need for improvement of the image of the quality of Japanese products. There was a desire to do this on a national level. Secondly the improvement in quality is started with the use of small group activities.

It is well known that Japanese goods were considered cheap in terms of quality and price. The shattered Japanese economy was to rebuild. The emphasis was given to improve the world market with the help of the United States. It became the main national objectives of Japanese scientists and engineer. The quality circles are accepted in nearly all industrial establishments. Thus, these quality circles have their foundation in Japanese industrial practice.

B) Definition :

Definition of quality circle is as follows :

1) **Ohmae :**

"Quality circle is a group of about 10 relatively autonomous workers from the same division of a company who volunteer to meet for an hour or so, once or twice a month. After work, they discuss the ways to improve the quality of their products, the production process in their part of the plant and the working environment. The long term objective is to build a sense of responsibility for improving quality but the immediate goal in to exchange ideas in a place uninhabited by barriers of age, sex or company rank."

C) Objectives of Quality Circle :

The main objectives of quality circles are as follows :

1) Promote the Development of Staff :

Quality Circles promote the development of staff. It is done by acquisition of new skills and the opportunity to work together. The problems are solved by discussions among themselves. They use their skills and abilities to solve the problems.

2) Helpful for Practical Framework :

It is helpful for the practical framework for introducing and developing participative management styles.

3) Programmes of the Organisation :

The quality circles aim at drawing programmes for the benefits of the organisation and the people in it. It helps in the development of healthier and more effective organisation.

4) Opportunity to Every Member :

It gives opportunity to every member to play their part actively.

5) Creation of Environment :

It creates an environment where workers are more conscious about quality problems and quality improvement.

6) Training of Staff :

To train people to understand and utilise their skills.

7) Encourage Participative Approach :

To encourage a participative approach to organisational problems.

D) Advantages of Quality Circle :

Following are the advantages of quality circle :

1) Use of Systematic Method :

Systematic method is used for problem solving as the problems are clearly defined by analysing the root causes by a group.

2) Participation of Everyone :

It involves the grassroot. Grassroot level gets involved in organisational problems.

3) Long Lasting Solutions :

Quality circles are permanent and long lasting solutions.

4) Probable Solution :

The use of the medium of Quality Circles is a probable solution.

E) Limitations of Quality Circle :

QCs have been criticized as a limited form of empowerment and a way to keep real decisions and control away from employees. QCs provide real benefits for both management and employees, but have significant limitations. These are following :

1) Limited Power :

Participants have limited power and can solve only certain types of problems in organizations. Because QCs have limited impact on traditional decision-making procedure, ability to involve workers in decision-making is also limited.

2) Not Practically Effective :

Also, Wood et al claimed that there is very little hard evidence for the claimed benefits of QCs. Griffin found significant differences between experimental QC groups and control groups for job satisfaction, organizational commitment, and performance rating. Head et al found QC group attitudes to actually decline over time, control group attitudes remaining constant. QCs are not practically effective when it comes to spearheading more participative management approaches in organizations.

3) Failure in Implementation :

Some circles try to deal with problem outside the member's areas of expertise thus reflecting poorly on the concept. The quality circle can come in with good ideas and management will fail to implement them.

4) Higher Position of Supervisor :

Some supervisors whose subordinates participate in quality circles believe their authority is usurped by the process. The employees might want to hold the higher position in the circles so he or she will being more respected than the others.

5) Lack Top Management Support :

Some circles lack top management support, although they have the support of lower level management, which they likely will result in their being less successful than they should or could be.

2.3.4 ISO-9000 :

Quality assurance indirectly means assurance of sales in the market. Inferior quality goods though available at low prices, generally rejected by the buyers. Qualities of product increase the competitive strength of companies. Such quality goods need no special advertisement and publicity. They occupy permanent place in the market and worldwide acceptance.

1) Concept of ISO-9000 :

ISO - 9000 is the foundation of Quality Management. It defines the minimum qualities of products, their standards for acceptability. It specifies the guidelines for implementing quality control measures. Again the quality system defines documents, procedures and responsibilities. It is regarded as responsibility of top management. These people (top management) decide the policy regarding quality of products and give commitments to customers.

2) Functions :

ISO - 9000 provides guidelines which are developed by expert's group who are representatives from 63 countries. ISO provides a check list against which an organisation can evaluate and improve its own internal quality system. ISO - 9000 quality standards define 20 sections relating to quality systems. The ISO - 9000 standards for quality management system are divided into six parts which are mainly the guidelines for managing quality rather than standards. These are not, however, the Government regulations and the standards set assure that customer's requirements will be fulfilled. To sum up, ISO - 9000 has been adopted widely in recent years in European country as well as in other 40 countries (including India) considering worldwide increasing competition as the result of liberalisation and globalisation of trading relations.

❋❋❋❋

Objective Type Questions

Q. I. Multiple Choice Questions :

1) Productivity = ------------.

a) Input / Output
b) Output / Input
c) Output – Input
d) Input – Output

2) Productivity is the ----------- of production system.

a) Measurement
b) Efficiency
c) Both (A) and (B)
d) None of the above

3) Productivity = ------------.

a) 1+ (Profit/Cost)
b) 1+ (Cost /Profit)
c) 1- (Profit/Cost)
d) 1- (Cost /Profit)

4) Productivity can be measured in which of the following input resource(s) ------------.

a) Material input
b) Labour input
c) Capital and Land Input
d) All of the above

5) Raw material productivity can be increased by ------------.

a) Proper choice of design
b) Reuse of material
c) Scrap control
d) All of the above

6) Productivity can be increased by ------------.

a) By increasing the output from the same input
b) By reducing the input for the same output
c) Both (A) and (B)

d) None of the above

7) The elimination of which of the following will improve industrial productivity?

a) Excess time
b) Ineffective time
c) Both (A) and (B)
d) None of the above

8) Process control is carried out ------------.

a) before production
b) during production
c) after production control
d) All of the above

9) Quality is ------------ variability.

a) opposite of
b) proportional to
c) reciprocal of
d) synonym of

10) Which one of these is a dimension of quality?

a) Performance
b) Hazard rate
c) Process Capability
d) Control limits

11) The function of quality control department is only the product of uniform and standard quality is allowed to be ------------.

a) Sold
b) Purchase
c) Both of the above
d) None of the above

12) Quality characteristics are classified into variables and ------------.

a) constants
b) attributes
c) standards
d) specifications

13) NPC stands for ------------.

a) National Productivity Council
b) Natural Productivity Council
c) National Public Council
d) National Productivity Country

14) Which formula correctly describes productivity?

a) (Output - Input)/Output
b) (Input - Output)/Input
c) Output/Input
d) Input/Output

15) If inputs decrease while output remains constant, what will happen to productivity?

a) It will increase.
b) It will decrease.
c) It will remain the same.
d) It is impossible to tell.

16) Which one of the following is not generally cited as a negative impact on productivity?

a) Government regulations
b) Liability claims
c) Increased emphasis on services
d) Emphasis on short-term performance
e) All are reasons.

17) A measure of productivity which reflects a combination of some or all of the resources used to obtain a certain output is ------------.

a) labor productivity
b) machine productivity
c) multi-factor productivity
d) materials productivity
e) overhead productivity

18) Counselling is a profession that aims to ------------.

a) Promote personal growth and productivity.
b) Provide a successful diagnosis in psychopathology.
c) Ensure that clients are on the correct medication.
d) Solely address behaviour.

19) What is credited with gains in industrial productivity, increased standards of living and affordable products?

a) personal computers
b) the internet
c) mass transportation
d) assembly lines

20) Which of the following is not a characteristic of service operations?

a) intangible output
b) high customer contact
c) high labor content
d) easy measurement of productivity

Ans : **1)** b, **2)** b, **3)** a, **4)** d, **5)** d, **6)** c, **7)** c, **8)** b, **9)** c, **10)** a, **11)** a, **12)** b, **13)** a, **14)** c, **15)** a, **16)** a, **17)** c, **18)** a, **19)** d, **20)** d.

Q. II. State the following statement are true or false :

1) Operations managers measure productivity as the ratio of input to output.
2) Productivity gains can curb inflation.
3) Standardizing processes can lead to increased productivity.
4) Productivity can be measured only on workers.
5) Productivity and efficiency are different names for the same thing.
6) Much of the responsibility for improving productivity rests with management.
7) Much of the responsibility for improving productivity rests with management.
8) The term total quality control was coined by Armand Fergenbaum.
9) The first step in the control process is the production of goods.
10) Control is both a process and an outcome.

Ans : **1)** False, **2)** True, **3)** True, **4)** False, **5)** False, **6)** True, **7)** True, **8)** True, **9)** False, **10)** True.

Review Questions

Q. 1. What are the factors that effect on the productivity of business?

Q. 2. Explain in detail the ways of measurement of productivity.

Q. 3. What do you mean by the term 'Productivity'? Discuss in detail about the importance of productivity.

Q. 4. Define the term Quality Circle. Explain in detail the objectives and limitations of the quality circle.

Q. 5. Explain the Importance of Productivity.

Q. 6. Explain the Objectives and Role of National Productivity Council.

Q. 7. **Write Short Notes on Following:**

a) Product Quality Control.

b) ISo-9000.

c) Limitations of Quality Circle.

❋❋❋❋

UNIT 3

Business Liasoning

- 3.1 Interface between Business and Government, Society and Natural Environment
- 3.2 Business Strategy

Introduction :

A business liaison is a trained professional who performs a variety of duties designed to maintain relationships, exchange information and promote operations. Below introduces some of the drastically different duties of business liaisons who can be found in almost every commercial sector. Business liaisons may work for a government agency and interface with private businesses, or they may represent corporations, businesses associations, commercial organizations with the government. These business liaisons will coordinate activities of certain departments, such as compliance, public relations and business development. For example, a government employed business liaison who works as a member of a business development team will act as a primary point of contact for new and existing businesses. They may provide referrals to business coaching, financing, licensing and real estate experts.

3.1 Interface between Business and Government, Society and Natural Environment :

Since businesses are strongly affected by public policies, it is in their best interest to stay informed about public policies and to try to influence governmental decision making and public policy. There are different general ways that businesses view and act on their relationship with government. One perspective is for businesses to consider business and government on "two sides" and in opposition to each other. Some have argued that this was the prevailing dominant mainstream business view in the aftermath of the Great Recession at the end of the first decade of the twenty-first century. It has been characterized as the "antiregulatory" or "limited government" view, and it has been associated with those who believe that free markets with a minimal government role is best for the workings of the economy. This perspective most often focuses businesses' interactions with government on efforts to minimize government and reduce the costs and burdens on private business and the general economy associated with government taxes, regulations, and policies. Environment is closely related with business. There is a constant 'give and take' relationship between environment and business. The business receives inputs, information and technology from the environment and gives it back in the form of outputs (goods and services).

3.1.1 Interface between Government and Business :

Government and businesses are the two most powerful institutions in any society. The two together determine public policy, both domestic and foreign, for a country. The policies, practices and regulations of the government influence to a large extent the nature, growth and functioning of the business system. In a situation of political stability business flourishes and businessmen venture to take greater risks. In the same way the ideology of the ruling party determines the nature and extent of economic development. If the ruling party believes in socialism, government control and ownership of business will grow. For example, public sector dominated development strategy in India until 1990. Major economic policies of a nation such as industrial policy, fiscal policy, monetary policy, and foreign trade policy are often based on political considerations. Several political decisions have strategic implications for business and industry. The term responsibility, accountability, obligation or duty is all used interchangeably in the context of relations between Government and business.

A) Responsibilities of Business towards Government :

The Government has certain definite expectation from business. The business houses are expected to fulfill the following responsibilities:

1) Regular Payment of Taxes :

Taxes are a major source of revenue for the Government. It is the responsibility of every businessman to pay regular taxes on sales, inputs and income. Moreover, it is the duty of the businessman, as an employer, to deduct the income tax from the salaries of the employees and remit the same to the government treasury.

2) Voluntary Programmes :

Another expectation of the Government from the business is that the business firms should cooperate with Government agencies on voluntary basis in connection with various programmes. Such as:

i) Sponsoring social welfare programmes
ii) Cultural growth
iii) Environmental preservation
iv) Promoting education
v) Population control measures

vi) Assistance in connection with drought relief etc.

Business does all this under the name of social responsibility.

3) Providing Information :

It is another responsibility of the business houses to give feedback information to the Government on the decisions taken by the political leaders. Business has necessary knowledge and experience. They can, therefore, place before the decision makers the facts and problems and argue for the modification or changes. This can be done by them individually or collectively.

4) Government Contracts :

Due to privatisation of the economy a number of Government contracts are executed by private business houses. Many business houses submit the tenders. It is the responsibility of the business houses to carry out the projects according to required specifications and standards.

5) Providing Service to the Government :

Sometimes, some influential and competent businessmen are included in the Advisory boards constituted by the Government. Some businessmen are appointed as members of the delegations who go abroad for exploring trade and industry prospectus.

6) Corporate Contributions to Political Activities :

The business houses are involved in the political activities in the following ways :

i) Making monetary contributions to political parties particularly at the time of elections.

ii) To contest elections as independents or on party tickets.

iii) Through lobbying, this refers to the behavior after the election and is concerned with securing legislation in favour of business.

It is the responsibility of the business houses to make sure that their political involvement provides an additional safeguard against the authoritarian potential of a mass society.

B) Responsibilities of Government towards Business :

The business has its own expectations from the Government. Specifically, the expectations of the business or the responsibilities of the Government towards business are as follows:

1) Political Institutions :

i) Government is responsible for preparing the laws which make the business system function smoothly. In these we include various economic and business laws.

ii) It is the responsibility of the Government to provide for the implementation of the laws.

iii) Further, it is the responsibilities of the Government to provide a proper judicial system for settling the disputes between business firms, individuals or Government agencies.

2) Provision of a Peaceful Atmosphere :

Government has the responsibility of maintaining law and order situation in the country and to provide protection to persons and their property. No successful business can be carried on in the absence of a peaceful atmosphere.

3) Provision of a System of Money and Credit :

The Government has to provide for a system of money and credit by means of which business transactions can be effected. Further, it is the responsibilities of the Government to regulate money and credit and to protect the money value of the rupee in terms of other currencies.

4) Balanced Development & Growth :

It is the responsibility of the Government to make sure that there is balanced regional development, full employment and a stable economy. Government has the resources and capabilities for all this; the only requirement is optimum utilisation of resources.

5) Provision of a Basic Infrastructure :

It is the responsibility of the Government to provide a basic infrastructure to the business this includes provision of banking, finance, transportation, power, trained personnel, warehousing and the other civil amenities.

6) Provision of Information :

It is the responsibility of the central, state and local Governments to provide information, which is useful to the businessman in conducting their business activities. This information may be about economic and business activity in general, specific lines of business, scientific and technological developments and many other things of interest to business houses.

7) To Assist Small Scale Industries :

The Government has special responsibility towards small scale industries because these industries generally face problems relating to finance, marketing, technical know-how and infrastructure. It is the responsibility of the Government to provide these facilities and to encourage small scale sector.

8) Transfer of Technology :

Another responsibility of the Government is that whatever discoveries are made by the Government owned research institutions should be transferred to private industry so that these can be used for commercial production.

9) Competition with Private Sector :

Government should compete with the private business firms for the purpose of ensuring healthy competition, improvement in the quality and regulating the prices.

10) Licensing and Inspections :

Government agencies should inspect the private business houses to ensure quality and to prohibit the sale of substandard goods. Moreover the Government should issue licenses to competent business establishments, so that they may carry on different and useful business activities.

11) Protection from Foreign Competition :

Government should encourage the development of home industries by providing them various subsidies and incentives. Moreover, measures like Tariffs and Quotas should be used by the Government to protect business from foreign competition.

To summarise we can say that the business should have complete faith in the ideologies of the Government. Similarly, the Government should have no inherent distrust against business in the private sector. The need of the hour is that the gap between the Government and business should be removed. There should be a spirit of partnership not one of reluctant association. We should learn a lesson from Japan where the relationship between Government and business is so close that the entire working of the Japanese economy is sometimes called "Japan Incorporated."

3.1.2 Interface between Business and Society :

The society is made up of different groups of stakeholders who affect or are affected by the actions of businesses, in different ways and different degrees; example includes but not limited to employees, customers, investors, suppliers, vendors, the government, etc.

Due to increased competition in today's market, business place high importance to maintaining good and lasting relationships with their stakeholders. To manage the interaction with these stakeholders, most businesses have created many departments to specifically interact with stakeholders and maintain the relationship with these stakeholders.

Based on system theory, corporations can be seen as a small piece or a small component of the entire integrated systems within a society involving political, social, economic, and environmental issues. Relating this with the systems theory, any changes made by an organization within its own company can have a positive or negative effect on any part of the political, social, economic or environmental system.

A) Business: An Integral Part of Society :

It is rather difficult to consider business and society as separate entities. Modern business has grown both in its reach and influence in society to such an extent that it has become an integral part of it. Both are influenced and affected by each other. Traditionally, the term business refers to activities such as buying or selling of goods and providing services with the objective of making profit. This implies that business refers to all the commercial activities that aim at making a profit for its owners or for organizations specially formed for that purpose. In recent times, however, there has been a substantial change in the manner in which business has been viewed by people. While earlier, the fundamental objective of business was considered profit-making, today profit is considered only secondary. In the present context society considers a business enterprise narrow-minded and myopic if its sole objective is only to make profit. Society views business as an integral part of the social system and believes that it has to sub-serve its interests. Business nowadays is, therefore defined as a "social institution performing a social mission and having a broad influence on the way people live and work together." It is now recognized that the direction of business is important to the public welfare and that businessmen perform a social function": Looked at from a broader angle, the term business covers a wide range of actions and institutions such as activities of small enterprises like a single owner tea-shop to giant corporation such as Tata Steel Ltd. as also those activities that include among other things, manufacturing, finance, trade and services.

B) Society, Values and Institutions :

Society generally refers to people in general or a nation or civilization, considered in relation to the laws, organizations, etc. that make it possible for them to live together. "Inherent in this concept of society are three fundamental interrelated parts: **(i)** ideas or beliefs; **(ii)** institutions; and **(iii)** material things.'" Ideas include attitudes, values, ideologies and beliefs, "which establish the broad goals of life expressed in terms of what is good, true, right, beautiful and acceptable." These beliefs and values are derived from a variety of sources including the mission of business as s social institution, the country in which these are evolved, the type of industry in which these are active and the quality and the value system of its employees. These values and beliefs inform and dominate the systems of institutional arrangements in the society, of which business is one. Institutions are formalized setups through which society tries to implement its goals or objectives through systems meant for business administration, politics, education, law and so on.

By material things, we mean the tangible things such as stocks of resources land and all manufactured goods which help shape and are partly products of our institutions, ideas and beliefs. "Our economic institutions together with our stock of resources, determine in large part the type and quantity of our material goods. As our types and quantities of material things change so do our ideas and beliefs."

C) The Interrelationship between Business and Society :

The interrelationship between business and the society is brought out by the fact that the former helps in the development and processing of certain economic values in the latter with the primary purpose of providing goods and services to the customers at a price marked in such a way as to earn a profit for the firm. However, making a profit may not be the sole aim of all economic and commercial activities in which a business enterprise is engaged. There are many non-commercial activities which do not end up in making a profit, such as activities of cooperative credit societies, charitable institutions like hospitals, orphanages and missionaries-run old- age homes, non-government organizations (NGOs) and institutions established solely for the purpose of promoting certain values in the society like thrift societies, sabhas to promote classical dance or music or those units engaged in creating awareness against smoking, HIV and for counseling such as Alcoholic Anonymous. These organizations also invest capital, produce or promote products or services manage their human resources without being involved in making profit. Thus, business today is viewed not merely as an institution to make profit. but as one which is a sub-system of the total social system with an objective larger and nobler than earning a profit.

D) Benefits of Business to Society :

Adam Smith argued that business firms in their attempts to maximize profits organize production by engaging and combining the various productive resources and coordinating them. Those who contribute the factors of production such as labour, capital and other resources are paid by the firms as a reward for their contribution. Thus, business enterprises generate income and employment for labour and owners of other factors of production. This benefits the society of which they are a considerable pan and contribute to their well-being. When what is produced is distributed to the ultimate consumers. The latter too gain from the increasing quantity and variety of goods and services produced for their consumption. Apart from the benefits that are conferred on the owners of resources and consumers. Business enterprises also contribute a great deal to governments revenues. Government impose taxes on profits the firms cam and impose a host of other levies all of which augment their revenue. These are used by them to provide public utility services undertake public welfare programmes and make investment for economic growth. It is, thus, seen that though the objective of a business firm is its own profit maximization it does contribute to the welfare of the society in innumerable ways and in a manner that appears different from its original objective of making profit for itself.

1) As a Promoter of Economic Growth :

A nation which is nothing but a political set up formed by society for the sake of convenience and for ensuring its functioning within a given law and order situation has to achieve faster economic growth if it has to offer for its people high standard of living and ensure their nature development. Economic growth is possible only with the contribution business makes to the society. If business is adequately unvested, well-organized, motivated and managed properly, it will flourish and add to the wealth, income and welfare of the society. If business does not flourish in a society, either due to unfriendly business policies of the government or poor patronage by the people, the prosperity of the nation would be at stake.

2) As a Contributor to Standard of Living of People :

The standard of living of people is directly related to (i) the income they have at their disposal and (ii) the amount of goods and services they are able to command and consume with their incomes. If people have a large amount of income, say, by exploiting abundant natural resources such as oil, but the society is not able to command considerable amounts of goods and services because their business has not developed, it will not add much to their standard of living. Since a nation's standard of living and welfare are directly related to its incomes and consumption levels, the role of business in augmenting both is indisputable.

3) As a Provider of Employment :

Full employment is one of the basic objectives of economic policies of governments. Any government worth its salt will have to ensure that all eligible and able-bodied persons willing to accept the existing level of wages are provided with employment opportunities. Employment alone provides income which is the wherewithal of consumption. Next to the external defense of the country, governments are concerned always about the problems relating to employment. And in this, the role of business is catalytic. Governments need the cooperation of business to provide employment to as many of its citizens as possible. Therefore, governments both in free-enterprise as well as socialist dispensations try to provide industry friendly policies to attract them to their states. The West Bengal government rules by Marxists have been going out of its way to woo industrialists to the state by offering several incentives. The huge economic stabilization package organized by governments all over the world running into more than USD 200 trillion is to boost business confidence and to avert low-demand-low-investment-low-production- low-income syndrome the traumatized business world experienced during the days of the Great Depression.

4) As a Source of Revenue to Modern Governments :

Business provides a significant source of revenue to modem governments. The sources of revenue to modern governments spring from four distinct streams, both direct and indirect, administrative revenues, commercial revenues and gifts and donations. Business has a pie in all these resources. Governments receive huge amounts of taxes through corporation tax, income tax from executives of business, excise duties imposed on goods produced, sales tax on goods and services sold, import duties, export duties, countervailing duties and a host of other imposts. Business also helps the government in its attempt to redistribute income to help the poor and the marginalized sections of the society increase their welfare. Governments in poor countries use their resources to provide public utility services, organize a public distribution system where goods are provided at highly subsidized rates to the poor and offer many public welfare programmes.

5) **As Participants in Projects to Promote Public Welfare :**
Business enterprises today have moved away from their original objective of only making profit so as to enrich the promoters and investors to get them actively involved in promoting the welfare of the society. This they do not only as an act of philanthropy, but also as active participants with other stakeholders in society to highlight social issues and find solutions to them.
Sometimes, business houses have been promoting activities supplementing the efforts of public authorities in certain areas that are important for all-round human development. Several corporations in India such as Tata Steel, ITC and the Srinivasan Services Trust of the TVS group of companies have been fighting environmental degradation and helping people to harmonize with nature by reducing pollution. Some companies have been adopting villages, helping physically and mentally challenged kids and go to the rescue and solace of people and communities ravaged by natural calamities such as earthquakes and tsunamis.
In recent times, many business organizations have taken to CSR as part of their business strategy to improve their performance and cam the goodwill of the society in the long run. Producers of dental or eye-care products organize mass clinics in villages and semi-urban areas where surgeons attend to medical needs of the poor and indigent. Incidentally, such attempts greatly relieve the burden on the finance-strapped state in a developing country like India where people, due to poverty and for historical reasons depend solely on the government to render every type of service.

6) **As Promoter and Protector of Stakeholders Interests :**
Business enterprises render a great deal of services to stakeholders who could be both insiders and outsiders. The insiders are employees and shareholders while outsiders include consumers, suppliers, creditors, competitors, government and the general public. Stakeholders in a business enterprise comprise almost all sections of the society, both as producers and consumers, employees and employers, creditors and borrowers and so on. Thus, if corporations promote the interests of all stakeholders, it promotes the welfare of the entire society.

E) **Problems Created by Business towards Society :**
In the process of their commercial activities, business enterprises create several problems especially when they are engaged in certain socially undesirable ways. Their activities impose certain social costs which are more than what benefits they have provided to it. Often, society has to spend enormous resources in regulating

and controlling business enterprises so as to prompt them to serve social interest and minimize harms done to it. Some of the problems that business firms have created in their attempt to make profit and how society has tried to regulate their activities with a view to ensuring that they work for public interest are discussed here.

1) Creation of Monopolies :

Business firms in their attempts to make huge profit at the cost of the consumer create monopolies in the production of some important products or services. Being monopolies, they exploit the consumers by creating artificial scarcities and charging higher prices and making excessive profits. In such instances, it becomes the duty of the government to regulate them. It has to fix fair prices for such commodities and services even while it ensures a fair return on investment to business firms. Governments also enact laws such as MKTP Act and establish bodies like the MRTP Commission in the course of regulating business.

2) Emergence of Oligopolies :

In free enterprise societies, emergence of oligopoly, i.e. a market dominated by a few, may be less than ten producers of a product compete with one other. In certain industries, such as cement, iron and steel and petroleum products in India, economies of scale are so large or barriers to entry into the industry are so strong that only a few firms provide these products to the market. With a view to making profit at the cost of the consumers, they formally or tactically collude with one another and form a cartel, thereby posing a threat to social interest. Such collusion among the few firms eliminates or substantially reduces competition through the formation of a cartel leading thereon to charging higher monopoly price and giving restricted output. On an international scale, Organization of Petroleum Exporting Countries (OPEC) is a classic example of such cartelization. Such collusion or formation of a cartel may be sought to be controlled by the society through enactment of anti-trust laws designed to prevent collusion among firms and creation of monopolies through mergers and sometimes by bringing in competition laws to promote competition.

3) Exploitation of Workers :

One of the most noticed undesirable activity of business enterprises is the exploitation of workers due to the existence of the unequal bargaining power between employers and workers. In India, as in many other poor countries where most of the workers are unorganized and there is a large pool of unemployed labour force, workers are exploited by being made to work for longer hours with low wages in unhygienic and unhealthy conditions and no social security benefits. Further, child and women labour are employed in private enterprises at very low wages while being made to work for longer hours and in hazardous occupations such as manufacturing of crackers. This has necessitated the regulation of business by the government fixing minimum wages payable to the workers. There are also laws which ban employment of child labour and requiring women to be paid equal wages as men, under the laws of equal pay for equal work. Likewise, there are laws that guarantee minimum wages for agricultural labour and other category of workers.

4) **Causing Environmental Degradation :**

Another serious adverse impact of business activity is the damage it causes to the environment. Traditionally, industry has been driven by consumer demand to produce goods, regardless of the consequences. Environmental pollution and ecological degradation caused by business and commercial activities impose heavy social cost on the economy and society. Industries dump their toxic waste into the air and water by polluting the atmosphere and poisoning water bodies. Such environmental pollution causes lung ailments, asthma, cancer and other health hazards apart from making agricultural lands until for cultivation. These are heavy social costs which the society bears, but the firms that have caused them do not share them. "Often, they do not provide safeguards so that undue smoke and other poisonous gases are emitted by them. Bhopal gas tragedy is a shining example of how private business limits neglect their social responsibility by not providing adequate safeguards for leakages and emission of poisonous gas."

5) **Corporate Greed Causing Worldwide Depression :**

Corporate greed and unethical practices followed by huge multinational corporations defies government regulations for observing corporate governance practices such as shareholder democracy, integrity and honesty in business operations, full financial and commercial disclosures and have resulted in harming not only themselves but national and global economies also. The recent Wall Street Crisis of 2008 has shown to what extent this kind of unmitigated greed for undeserved profit has led the entire global economy into a meltdown forcing governments of not only advanced economies like the US and England but of low-income economies such as China and India also release trillions of dollars for creating liquidity into the financial system and pulling out their economies from depression.

6) **Unethical Practices :**

Businesses have also been a major cause of corruption and bribery in society. Many of them adopt unethical, illegal and fraudulent practices to achieve faster growth and greater market share. Big businesses have used their money power and economic clout to buy political influence, bend rules and regulations and even prompt enactment of laws to help in their growth. "Corruption in industry which is a major by-product of degradation of values and ethics is also related to the inability of industry to stand up to the discretionary powers of a regulatory system designed and administered by an unholy alliance of bureaucrats and politicians." Indian economic history since Independence is replete with examples of family promoted corporations enjoying astronomical growth by following such unethical practices. Though these practices inflict heavy social costs, it is rare that they are detected and their perpetrators penalized by authorities.

3.1.3 Interface between Business and Environment :

Both the environment and business are interrelated and interdependent on each other for its survival and growth. Both cannot- exist without each other. Business to run successfully has to adjust with the changing environment. Both business and environment are closely related concepts. The interface between business and various types of environment can be briefly explained with the following points :

1) Business and Demographic Environment :

Demography is the study of human population with reference to their age, gender, status, occupation, income, education etc. The demographic environment differs from country to country and has significant implications on business. On the other hand business firm also affect the demographic pattern of a country. Due to diversified demographic environment, a business is compelled to adopt different functional and marketing strategies.

For example:

Business undertakes various social welfare programmes like health camps, awareness, and literacy programmes etc. In the same way rise in the income level of consumers helps in rise in demand for products.

The business undertakes research activities to turn the potential customers into final customers with reference to their age, gender, income, status, qualification etc. for undertaking production, marketing and promotional activities. The business firm has to adjust with the changing demographic pattern of the country.

2) Business and Economic Environment :

The economic environment of a country comprises of the structure of the economy, economic resources, level of income, economic policies etc. Any change in the economic policy can have a positive or negative impact on the working of the business. Business organisation has to consider the various economies prevailing in the country like import policy, industrial policy, taxation policy etc. which can have a great impact on the business. Economic policies like liberalisation, privatisation, and globalisation had a considerable impact on the business. Changes in the economic policy ultimately affect the business. For example: change in the income structure of the consumers will ultimately affect their purchasing power and sale of the organisation.

Increase in the income well result into growth of organisational sale and vice versa. Favourable economic environment helps in rise in the national income and increase in the standard of living.

Favourable economic environment also facilitates increase in foreign direct investment and growth of industrial sector resulting into growth of economy as a whole.

The business should study the economic environment to understand the market conditions, international events, to analyses investment policies, competitor's policies, economic policies of government etc.

3) **Business and Technological Environment :**

Technology refers to the set of process in an organisation to transform raw material of resources into finished goods and services. Technology includes tools- both machine (hard technology) and way of thinking (soft technology).

It includes not only the knowledge and method but also the entrepreneurial expertise that enhances the competitiveness of a nation. Technology can greatly influence business decisions. It helps in minimizing cost, reducing wastage and brings higher efficiency in the production process. Information technology has brought about revolutionary changes in the world of business environment.

On the other hand business is responsible for technological up gradation as a huge amount is spent on Research and Development to introduce new products and concepts in the business. This technological revolution became a compelling reason for internationalization and Globalisation. Quick adoption of latest technology will help the business to gain competitive advantage and facilitates overall industrial efficiency.

4) **Business and Natural Environment :**

Both natural environment and business are closely related and have influence over each other. Natural environment is also termed as physical environment Business depends on the nature for supply of resources like raw material, water etc.

The business has to adjust with the environment to ensure its survival. Ecological factors have recently assumed great importance. The excessive use of these resources, environmental pollution and the disturbance of ecological balance has caused great concern. One cannot take the environment granted.

The business should give due consideration for the conservation of natural resources. Similarly geographical factors affect the location of industries. Availability of natural resources is the fundamental factor in the development of industries.

Weather and climatic conditions affect the demand pattern. Manufacturing the most important aspect of business depends upon physical environment. Thus natural environment has a great influence on the economic activities. Similarly environment is also depended upon the business. Business should produce pollution free products and service to keep the environment pollution free and maintain the ecological balance.

5) Business and Cultural Environment :

Culture refers to values, attitude, belief, morals, customs and traditions. Culture is a critical component of business environment. Proper understanding of cultural dimension is very important for product development, promotion, human resource management etc. Business and culture are closely associated with each other. Culture is the powerful element to shape the business. The business should come up with various cultural events, thereby promoting and preserving the rich culture of a country.

Business should be well versed with the culture, language, traditions shared by different community to meet their wants. Understanding of culture is very essential in the formulation of business strategies. As culture influence business activities, business also should influence our culture by promoting festivals and cultural events in the country.

▶ 3.2 Business Strategy :

Business strategy is vital for any company seeking to grow its business in a strategic manner, but what exactly is a business strategy? Put simply, it's a clear set of plans, actions and goals that outlines how a business will compete in a particular market, or markets, with a product or number of products or services. But while simple to understand in theory, developing a good business strategy- and then actually implementing it - is no easy task.

3.2.1 Meaning :

Business strategy can be understood as the course of action or set of decisions which assist the entrepreneurs in achieving specific business objectives. It is nothing but a master plan that the management of a company implements to secure a competitive position in the market, carry on its operations, please customers and achieve the desired ends of the business.

A business strategy can be defined as the combination of all the decisions taken and actions performed by the business to accomplish business goals and to secure a competitive position in the market. It is the backbone of the business as it is the roadmap which leads to the desired goals. Any fault in this roadmap can result in the business getting lost in the crowd of overwhelming competitors.

3.2.2 Importance of Business Strategy :

A Business strategy map is a great way to put out the whole picture on a piece of paper and to make tweaks and adjustments to business activities to achieve the vision and goals of the company. Everything in an enterprise is interrelated and having a defined business strategy makes the whole thing clear-where you need to work the most and where you need the least amount of work. Every business needs a strategy something to outline the shared goals of their organisation. A well-outlined business strategy is essential for the success and sustainability of any business venture. Without one, organisations can lack direction, efficiency and profitability. Importance of business strategy is as follows :

1) **Planning :**

   Business strategy is a part of a business plan. While the business plan sets the goals and objectives, the strategy gives you a way to fulfill those goals. It is a plan to reach where you intend to.

2) **Strengths & Weaknesses :**

   Most of the times, you get to know about your real strengths and weaknesses while formulating a strategy. Moreover, it also helps you capitalise on what you're good at and use that to overshadow your weaknesses (or eliminate them).

3) **Efficiency & Effectiveness :**

   When every step is planned, every resource is allocated, and everyone knows what is to be done, business activities become more efficient and effective automatically.

4) **Competitive Advantage :**

   A business strategy focuses on capitalising on the strengths of the business and using it as a competitive advantage to position the brand in a unique way. This gives an identity to business and makes it unique in the eyes of the customer.

5) **Control :**

   It also decides the path to be followed and interim goals to be achieved. This makes it easy to control the activities and see if they are going as planned.

3.2.3 Steps in Developing Business Strategies :

The business goal is achieved by the effective execution of different business strategies. While every employee, partner, and stakeholder of the company focus on fulfilling a single business objective, their activities are defined by various business strategies according to their level in the organisation. Following are the steps in developing business strategies:

1) **Develop a True Vision :**

   Vision is an abstract word that means different things to different people. Classically, a vision or vision statement is a snapshot into the future. It should include aspirations of what type of company you want to be, and, unlike a mission statement, articulates what success looks like in clear terms (customers, markets, volume, etc.)

2) **Define Competitive Advantage :**

   At the essence of strategy is identifying how a company can deliver unique value to its customers. In many sectors of the economy, companies are stuck in a sea of sameness. A well-thought-out business strategy should consider how a company can create space from competition in its service offering, pricing model, delivery system and more.

3) **Define Business Targets :**

   One of the most significant barriers to growth is poor targeting. Absent of very specific targets, companies suffer from unclear messaging and thus misalignment between sales and marketing. Defining niches and specialties allows companies to focus resources (of course, some companies are generalists by design).

Clear target markets give a company the ability to create an integrated sales and marketing approach, where marketing enables sales productivity. Sales and marketing plans are executed more effectively when targets are tight.

4) Focus on Systematic Growth :

As one of our Vistage member clients says, "A thriving company is a growing company." It is only through growth that companies can afford to invest in things like technology, the best people and new equipment. The strategic plan should identify in which segments a company will grow and in what proportion, so that the product mix yields a specific net margin result. Only after coming to such conclusions could a company knows how much it can afford in terms of capex, overhead expenses and so on.

5) Make Fact-based Decisions :

Strategy is garbage in, garbage out exercise. Executives often complain about a lack of good data, but we consistently find information that is useful in the formation of strategy. We once worked with a Vistage member who was trying to quantify the value of various segments served. By accessing the public records of a nearby port, we were able to quantify actual shipments of merchandise by potential customers.

6) Think Long Term :

In the face of constant change, planning horizons are shorter than they used to be. However, only thinking quarter to quarter is a trap that may rob companies of their ability to see around the bend. Best-in-class companies create processes designed to treat strategy as an annual cycle rather than a one-time, static event.

7) But, be Nimble :

Companies can think long term and still be nimble. For example, a critical component of strategy is an external forces analysis. Companies should be evaluating long-term external forces, and adapting based on new information (meeting regularly-perhaps quarterly) to pivot.

8) Be Inclusive :

To be nimble, companies are including different people in their strategy than in the past. At a time when companies are hiring more millennial employees, there is greater transparency.

9) Invest time in Pre-work :

If you want your managers to take strategy seriously, make them conduct research and prepare relevant information in advance of your strategy meetings.

10) Performance Management :

All the planning and hard work may have been done, but it's vital to continually review all objectives and action plans to make sure you're still on track to achieve that overall goal. Managing and monitoring a whole strategy is a complex task, which is why many directors, managers and business leaders are looking to alternative methods of handling strategies. Creating, managing and reviewing a strategy requires you to capture the relevant information, break down large chunks of information, plan, prioritise, capture the relevant information and have a clear strategic vision.

3.2.4 Components of Business Strategy :

While an objective is defined clearly in the business plan, the strategy answers all what's, why's, who's, where's, when's, & how's of the fulfilling that objective. Here are the key components of a business strategy.

1) **Mission, Vision, & Business Objectives :**

   The main focus of a business strategy is to fulfil the business objective. It gives the vision and direction to the business with clear instructions of what needs to be done, how it needs to be done, and who all are responsible for it.

2) **Core Values :**

   It also states the 'musts' and 'must nots' of the business which clarify most of the doubts and give a clear direction to the top level, units, as well as the departments.

3) **SWOT :**

   A SWOT (strengths, weaknesses, opportunities, and threats) analysis is a rundown of the company's current situation. It is a necessary component of a business strategy as it represents the current strengths and opportunities which the company can make use of and the weaknesses and threats which the company should be wary of.

4) **Operational Tactics :**

   Unit and functional business strategies get deep into the operational details of how the work needs to be done in order to be most effective and efficient. This saves a lot of time and effort as everyone knows what needs to be done.

5) **Resource Procurement & Allocation Plan :**

   The strategy also answers where and how will you procure the required resources, how will it be allocated, and who will be responsible for handling it.

6) **Measurement :**

   Unless there are no control measures, the viability of a business strategy can't be assessed properly. A good business strategy always includes ways to track the company's output and performance against the set targets.

Objective Type Questions

Q. I. Multiple Choice Questions :

1) **Which one of the following cannot be included under the nature of relationship between business and environment?**
   a) Interdependence b) Dynamic
   c) Social change d) Fixed
2) **------------ environment is within the control of the business.**
   a) Internal b) External c) Micro d) Macro
3) **Which item does not cause any business risk?**
   a) Breakdown of machinery b) Efficient management
   c) Riot d) Changing government policy
4) **The nature and power of a statutory corporation is defined in ------------.**
   a) Special statute b) Companies Act 2013
   c) Both a & b d) None of the above
5) **A government company is any company in which the paid-up capital held by the government is not less than ------------.**
   a) 49% b) 50% c) 25% d) 51%
6) **Which company having business operation in more than one country?**
   a) Multinational Company b) Departmental Undertaking
   c) Statutory Corporation d) Government Company
7) **If business is to operate in a society which is full of diverse and complicated problems, it may have ------------.**
   a) Little chance of success b) Great chance of success
   c) Little chance of failure d) No relation with success or failure
8) **The economic environment of a business includes ------------.**
   a) Economic system b) Economic policies
   c) Economic conditions d) All of these
9) **Which strategy is about how to compete successfully in particular markets?**
   a) Business-level strategy b) Corporate-level strategy
   c) Alliance-based strategy d) Operational-level strategy
10) **Business Strategy should be formulated keeping in a mind a time horizon of ------------.**
    a. 3 - 5 years b. 3 -6 months
    c. less than one year d. None of these
11) **Business Success hinges on the capability of a firm to ------------.**
    a) formulate and execute action plans b) Craft Internal plans
    c) Allocate Resources efficiently d) predict the internal environment

12) The strategy of TATA Motors and TCS would be classified as ------------.

a) Corporate Strategy b) Business Strategy

c) Operational Strategy d) Process Level

13) strategy can be defined as ------------.

a) Operational plans

b) Line and direction followed by a firm

c) Plans designed irrespective of the environmental conditions

d) Integrated Broad set of action plans cutting across all business functions

14) Which of the following defines how each individual business unit will attempt to achieve its mission?

a) Business strategy b) Corporate strategy

c) Functional strategy d) National strategy

15) A strategy is derived from ------------.

a) Policy b) Objective c) Method d) Rule

16) The task of strategy choice involves ------------.

a) developing plans and activities which will improve the organisation's performance and competitive position

b) determining how the organisation can be more market and efficiency oriented

c) monitoring whether the organisation is achieving good financial performance

d) keeping the organisation free of debt

17) Which of the following is not a stage of strategy formulation techniques?

a) Formulation Framework b) Matching stage

c) External factor evaluation d) Decision stage

18) A strategy is a company's ------------.

a) Value statement b) Pricing policy

c) Game Plan to outsmart competitor d) Long-term objective

19) Strategy-formulation concepts and tools ------------.

a) Do not differ greatly for different size and type of organizations

b) Differ greatly for different size and type of organizations

c) Do not differ greatly for profit or non-profit organizations but differ in small and large organizations

d) None of the mentioned options

20) Strategy evaluation at the ------------ level involves using specific performance measures-qualitative and quantitative-for each functional area.

a) organizational b) operational c) functional d) production

Ans : **1)** d, **2)** a, **3)** d, **4)** a, **5)** d, **6)** a, **7)** a, **8)** d, **9)** a, **10)** a, **11)** a, **12)** b, **13)** d, **14)** a, **15)** b, **16)** a, **17)** b, **18)** c, **19)** a, **20)** c.

Q. II. State the following statement are true or false :

1) Business is not important for the society.
2) A business is an activity started for the purpose of profit.
3) Currently, there is a lack of interest in the importance "of the social responsibility of business.
4) It is important to recognize that strategy is not only a process, but also a way of thinking.
5) A successful strategy can be realized only if the management and employees are committed, necessary resources are allocated, and a supportive culture and environment are provided.
6) Business level strategy making is the responsibility of the firm's board of directors, who have to respond to the shareholders of the firm.
7) Strategy requires the firm to match the choice of competitive methods with the opportunities in the environment and to allocate its resources to those methods that generate the highest level of cash flow per share of equity.
8) Once the corporate strategy determines what businesses the firm will be engaged in, the decision must then be made on acquiring another or building a new business.
9) Strategic factors are those external and internal elements that will determine the future of the corporation.
10) Strategy implementation includes the allocation of resources needed to implement the strategy.

Ans : **1)** False, **2)** True, **3)** True, **4)** False, **5)** True, 6) False, 7) True, 8) False, **9)** True, **10)** True.

Review Questions

Q. 1. Discuss in detail about the Interface between Government and Business.

Q. 2. Explain in detail about the Interface between Business and Society.

Q. 3. Discuss in detail about the Interface between Business and Natural Environment.

Q. 4. Explain in detail about the Responsibilities of Business towards Government.

Q. 5. Explain the Responsibilities of Government towards Business.

Q. 6. What do you mean by Business Strategy? Explain the Importance of Business Strategy.

Q. 7. Write Short Notes on Following:

a) The Interrelationship between Business and Society.

b) Problems Created by Business towards Society.

c) Business and Technological Environment.

d) Steps in Developing Business Strategy.

e) Components of Business Strategy.

Business Alliance (Growth Strategies)

UNIT 4

- ▶ 4.1 Businesss Alliance
- ▶ 4.2 Growth Strategies - Expansion
- ▶ 4.3 Integration and Diversification
- ▶ 4.4 Mergers and Acquisition
- ▶ 4.5 Franchising
- ▶ 4.7 Public Private Partnership

▶ Introduction :

A business alliance, also known as a strategic alliance, is a formal business relationship between two or more organizations that share similar short and long-term objectives. A business alliance structure can include joint ventures, franchising, cross-licensing, cross-marketing, and co-manufacturing. A business alliance is an agreement between businesses, usually motivated by cost reduction and improved service for the customer. Alliances are often bounded by a single agreement with equitable risk and opportunity share for all parties involved and are typically managed by an integrated project team. Business Alliances are designed to help existing businesses grow, help communities attract new jobs, and provide increased training opportunities for business owners and residents. The Business Alliance program takes advantage of the flexibility of the private sector and provides a way for the business community to develop mutually beneficial partnerships. These partnerships reflect the unique characteristics of a business community and the perspectives of business owners who are most directly affected by revitalization efforts and whose participation and cooperation are critical. The Business Alliance brings together public and private groups and individuals who are enthusiastic about fostering real economic change in their communities.

4.1 Business Alliance :

Joint ventures involve two or more companies forming a new company to pursue a common objective. Strategic partnerships involve two or more companies sharing resources, knowledge, and capabilities to achieve a common goal. Supplier-buyer relationships involve a supplier providing products or services to a buyer, while licensing agreements allow one company to use another company's intellectual property in exchange for a fee. Distribution agreements allow one company to distribute another company's products or services.

Business alliances are often formed to gain a competitive advantage, reduce costs, increase market share, or expand into new markets. By combining their resources and expertise, businesses can achieve these goals more effectively than they would be able to on their own.

Successful business alliances require careful planning, open communication, and a shared vision. It is important for each partner to understand and respect the other's strengths and weaknesses and to work together to overcome any obstacles that arise. By building a strong, collaborative relationship, businesses can create long-term value and achieve sustainable growth.

4.1.1 Meaning :

A business alliance is a collaborative relationship between two or more businesses or organizations for mutual benefit. Business alliances are formed to achieve common goals that could not be achieved by a single entity or to create synergies that enhance each partner's competitive position.

Alliances can take many different forms and can be established between companies in the same industry or in different industries. Some common forms of business alliances include joint ventures, strategic partnerships, supplier-buyer relationships, licensing agreements, and distribution agreements.

In a business alliance, each partner brings its unique strengths, resources, and expertise to the table to create a mutually beneficial arrangement.

Business alliances can take many forms, such as joint ventures, marketing partnerships, distribution partnerships, supply chain partnerships, and technology partnerships. For example, a distribution partnership between two companies might involve one company providing the other with access to its distribution network in exchange for the other company's products or services.

The benefits of business alliances can include increased market share, expanded distribution channels, shared costs and risks, enhanced product or service offerings, and access to new markets or technologies. However, it's important to choose the right partner, establish clear objectives and expectations, and maintain good communication and trust throughout the partnership to ensure its success.

4.1.2 Definitions :

1) A business alliance is a strategic relationship between two or more independent businesses that collaborate to achieve mutual goals, share resources and knowledge, and gain a competitive advantage.
2) A business alliance is a formal agreement between two or more businesses to work together in a mutually beneficial way. The alliance may be formed to gain access to new markets, leverage technology, share resources, or reduce costs.
3) A business alliance is a partnership between two or more companies to collaborate on a specific project or to achieve a specific goal. Alliances are typically formed to leverage complementary strengths, share risks and costs, and gain a competitive advantage.

4.1.3 Importance of Business Alliance :

Importance of Business Alliance are as follows :

1) **Access to New Markets :**

   A business alliance can provide access to new markets and customer bases that may be difficult or costly to reach on your own. By partnering with another business that has a strong presence in a particular market, you can expand your reach and increase your sales.

2) **Shared Resources and Expertise :**

   A business alliance can allow you to share resources, knowledge, and expertise with your partner, which can help you reduce costs, improve efficiency, and accelerate innovation. By pooling your resources, you can achieve more than you would be able to on your own.

3) **Risk Sharing :**

   Business alliances can help you share risks and costs with your partner, which can reduce your exposure to potential losses. By partnering with another business, you can share the financial burden of a project or initiative, making it less risky for both parties.

4) **Competitive Advantage :**

   A business alliance can give you a competitive advantage by allowing you to leverage your partner's strengths and expertise. By collaborating with another business, you can combine your complementary strengths to create a unique value proposition that sets you apart from your competitors.

5) **Strategic Growth :**

   Business alliances can be a strategic way to fuel your growth and expansion plans. By partnering with another business, you can tap into their resources and expertise to help you achieve your growth objectives more quickly and efficiently.

▶ 4.2 Growth Strategies-Expansion :

Growth strategies refer to the various methods and approaches used by businesses to expand their operations, increase their market share, and improve their financial performance. The objective of growth strategies is to enable businesses to reach their full potential by generating more revenue, profits, and customer loyalty.

4.2.1 Growth Strategies :

Growth Strategies are as follows :

A) Different Growth Strategies :

There are several different growth strategies that businesses can pursue, including :

1) Market Penetration :

This involves increasing market share by selling more products or services to existing customers or by acquiring new customers in the same market.

2) Market Development :

This involves expanding the company's operations into new markets, either by selling the same products or services to a new customer segment or by introducing new products or services into an existing market.

3) Product Development :

This involves creating and introducing new products or services to an existing market, either to meet changing customer needs or to gain a competitive advantage.

4) Diversification :

This involves expanding the company's operations into new product or service lines that are different from the existing offerings, either to spread the risk or to take advantage of new growth opportunities.

5) Acquisition :

This involves acquiring other companies to gain access to their resources, technology, customers, or market share.

B) Advantages of Growth Strategies for Businesses :

Advantages of Growth Strategies for Businesses are as follows :

1) Increased Revenue and Profits :

Growth strategies aim to increase the size of the business, which can lead to higher revenue and profits. By expanding the customer base, introducing new products or services, or entering new markets, businesses can generate more sales and revenue, leading to higher profits.

2) Improved Brand Recognition :

Growth strategies, such as geographical expansion, acquisition, and partnership, can help businesses increase their brand recognition and reputation. This can enhance the company's image, customer loyalty, and market competitiveness.

3) Economies of Scale :

As businesses grow and expand their operations, they can benefit from economies of scale, which means that the cost per unit decreases as the volume of production or sales increases. This can result in increased efficiency, lower costs, and higher profitability.

4) Diversification :

Pursuing growth strategies, such as product or market diversification, can help businesses spread their risk and reduce dependence on a single product or market. This can improve the company's resilience to economic downturns or changes in the market.

5) Increased Bargaining Power :

As businesses grow and expand, they can increase their bargaining power with suppliers, customers, and other stakeholders. This can lead to better pricing, better terms, and more favorable relationships with partners and suppliers.

C) Disadvantages of Growth Strategies for Businesses :

Disadvantages of Growth Strategies for Businesses are as follows :

1) Increased Risk :

Pursuing growth strategies involves taking on new challenges, such as entering new markets, introducing new products or services, or acquiring other businesses. These activities can be risky, and the business may not always achieve the expected results, which can lead to financial losses.

2) Resource Constraints :

Pursuing growth strategies requires significant resources, such as funding, management expertise, and staff. Businesses may need to invest heavily in research and development, marketing, and infrastructure to support growth, which can strain resources and distract from the core operations of the business.

3) Reduced Focus :

Pursuing growth strategies can distract the business from its core operations and lead to a loss of focus. This can result in a decline in the quality of the products or services and the loss of customer loyalty.

4) Organizational Challenges :

As businesses grow, they may face new organizational challenges, such as increased bureaucracy, communication breakdowns, and difficulties in maintaining the company culture. These challenges can result in decreased employee morale, productivity, and job satisfaction.

5) Integration issues :

Pursuing growth strategies, such as acquisition or partnership, can lead to integration issues with the new businesses or partners. This can result in cultural clashes, disagreements on strategy or management, or difficulties in integrating different systems or processes.

4.2.2 Expansion :

Expansion is a common growth strategy for businesses, which involves increasing their market reach, sales, and revenue by expanding their operations, products, or services. There are several ways in which a company can expand its business, including:

1) **Geographical Expansion :**
   This involves expanding the business to new geographical locations. A company can open new stores, offices, or production facilities in new locations, or it can enter new markets by exporting products or services to other countries.
2) **Product Expansion :**
   This involves expanding the product or service offerings of a company. This can be achieved by introducing new products or services, improving existing ones, or diversifying the product or service line.
3) **Acquisition :**
   This involves acquiring another business to expand the company's operations, customer base, or product offerings. This can be a quick way to expand a business, but it also comes with risks and challenges.
4) **Partnership :**
   This involves forming partnerships with other companies to expand the business. This can involve co-branding, joint ventures, or strategic alliances.
5) **Franchising :**
   This involves expanding the business by franchising the company's brand and business model to other entrepreneurs who can open their own franchises.

▶ 4.3 Integration and Diversification :

Integration and Diversification are as follows :

4.3.1 Integration:

In the context of business alliances, integration refers to the process of combining the resources, expertise, and capabilities of two or more companies to create value and achieve common objectives. Business alliances can take many forms, such as joint ventures, strategic partnerships, mergers, and acquisitions.

Integration in business alliances involves bringing together the different elements of each partner company, such as their products, services, employees, and culture, to form a cohesive whole. This can be a complex and challenging process, as each company may have different goals, strategies, and ways of doing things.

The integration process typically involves several stages, such as planning, due diligence, negotiation, implementation, and monitoring. During the planning stage, the partners must identify the potential synergies and risks of the alliance and develop a roadmap for achieving their objectives. During due diligence, the partners must thoroughly investigate each other's financial, legal, and operational aspects to ensure that the alliance is viable and sustainable.

Negotiation involves setting the terms and conditions of the alliance, such as ownership structure, management, governance, and decision-making. Implementation involves putting the alliance into action, such as integrating the companies' systems, processes, and employees. Monitoring involves assessing the performance of the alliance and making adjustments as needed to ensure that it remains aligned with the partners' objectives.

Successful integration in business alliances can bring many benefits, such as increased market share, enhanced innovation, reduced costs, and improved competitive position. However, it requires a high level of collaboration, trust, and communication between the partners, as well as a shared vision and commitment to the alliance's success.

A) Importance of Integration in Business Alliances:

Importance of Integration in Business Alliances are as follows :

1) Synergy :

Integration can help to create synergy between the partners, which can result in greater efficiency, productivity, and profitability. By combining resources, expertise, and capabilities, partners can achieve more together than they could individually.

2) Alignment :

Integration can also help to align the partners' goals and objectives, which is critical for the success of any alliance. By ensuring that both partners are on the same page and working towards the same end, integration can help to prevent conflicts and ensure a smooth working relationship.

3) Standardization :

Integration can help to standardize processes and procedures across the partners, which can help to eliminate duplication of effort and reduce costs. This can also help to improve the quality of the products or services provided by the alliance.

4) Customer Focus :

Integration can help to create a more customer-focused approach, which is essential for any successful business. By combining the strengths of the partners, the alliance can create a more complete and comprehensive solution for its customers, which can result in greater customer satisfaction and loyalty.

5) Risk Mitigation :

Integration can also help to mitigate risks associated with business alliances. By creating a more unified and cohesive entity, the partners can better manage risks and respond to potential challenges.

B) Disadvantages of Business Alliances :

Disadvantages of Business Alliances are as follows :

1) Loss of Autonomy :

Integration can result in the loss of autonomy for the partners, as they must work together in a more coordinated and collaborative way. This can be challenging for partners who are used to operating independently and making their own decisions.

2) Cultural Differences :

Integration can also highlight cultural differences between the partners, which can lead to conflicts and misunderstandings. Differences in management style, work ethic, and communication style can all impact the success of the alliance.

3) Resistance to Change :

Integration can also be met with resistance from employees and other stakeholders who may be resistant to change or feel threatened by the alliance. This can result in a lack of buy-in and enthusiasm for the alliance, which can hinder its success.

4) Integration Costs :

Integration can be costly, both in terms of time and money. Integrating processes, systems, and teams can be time-consuming and require significant resources to implement successfully.

5) Loss of Competitive Advantage :

Integration can also result in the loss of competitive advantage, as the partners may be sharing proprietary information or knowledge that they would otherwise keep private. This can result in the loss of their unique selling points, which can impact their market position.

4.3.2 Diversification :

Diversification is a risk management strategy that involves spreading investments across different asset classes, industries, regions, and other categories. The goal of diversification is to reduce the overall risk of an investment portfolio by ensuring that no single asset or group of assets can significantly impact the portfolio's performance.

The theory behind diversification is that different types of assets tend to perform differently in different market conditions. For example, stocks may perform well in a bull market, while bonds may perform better during a bear market. By holding a mix of different assets, an investor can potentially reduce the volatility of their portfolio and improve its long-term performance.

Diversification can be achieved through a variety of investment vehicles, including stocks, bonds, mutual funds, exchange-traded funds (ETFs), real estate, and alternative investments such as commodities or private equity. A well-diversified portfolio will typically include a mix of these different asset classes, with the specific allocation depending on the investor's risk tolerance, investment goals, and other factors.

A) Importance of Diversification :

Importance of Diversification are as follows :

1) Reducing Risk :

One of the most significant benefits of diversification is that it helps to reduce the risk of loss in an investment portfolio. By spreading investments across different asset classes and sectors, investors can avoid the impact of a single market downturn or event. This can help to protect the portfolio from significant losses.

2) Improving Returns :

Diversification can also help to improve portfolio returns over the long term. By investing in a mix of assets that perform differently under different market conditions, investors can potentially smooth out volatility and generate more consistent returns.

3) Enhancing Liquidity :

Diversification can also help to enhance portfolio liquidity, making it easier to buy and sell assets as needed. This is because a well-diversified portfolio typically includes a mix of assets with different levels of liquidity, from highly liquid investments such as stocks to less liquid investments such as real estate.

4) Managing Emotions :

Diversification can help investors to manage their emotions and avoid making impulsive investment decisions based on short-term market movements. By holding a mix of assets, investors are less likely to be influenced by the ups and downs of any single asset class.

5) Achieving Investment Goals :

Diversification is an essential part of achieving long-term investment goals. A well-diversified portfolio can help investors to build wealth, generate income, and preserve capital over the long term.

B) Disadvantages of Diversification :

Disadvantages of Diversification are as follows :

1) Reduced Returns in a Single Asset Class :

One potential disadvantage of diversification is that it can limit the potential returns of a single asset class. If a particular asset class is experiencing strong growth, a diversified portfolio may not benefit as much as a concentrated portfolio that is solely invested in that asset class.

2) Higher Transaction Costs :

Diversification often involves investing in a larger number of assets, which can result in higher transaction costs and fees. This can reduce the net returns of the portfolio over time.

3) Difficulty in Monitoring Investments :

A well-diversified portfolio can be challenging to monitor and manage effectively. This is because it requires keeping track of a larger number of investments across different asset classes and sectors.

4) Over-diversification :

Over-diversification is another potential disadvantage of diversification. When a portfolio is too diversified, it can become challenging to manage and can result in lower returns. Over-diversification can also increase transaction costs and make it more difficult to monitor investments effectively.

5) Exposure to Systemic Risk :

While diversification can help to mitigate the risk of individual assets or sectors, it may not protect against systemic risk that affects the broader economy or financial markets. In some extreme scenarios, such as a severe recession or market crash, a diversified portfolio may still experience significant losses.

▶ 4.4 Mergers and Acquisition :

Mergers and acquisitions (M&A) are defined as consolidation of companies. Differentiating the two terms, Mergers is the combination of two companies to form one, while Acquisitions is one company taken over by the other. M&A is one of the major aspects of corporate finance world. The reasoning behind M&A generally given is that two separate companies together create more value compared to being on an individual stand. With the objective of wealth maximization, companies keep evaluating different opportunities through the route of merger or acquisition.

4.4.1 Mergers :

Business combinations are a new trend in expansion of business. There is integration of competing business units in combinations. Mergers and acquisitions are combinations of two or more business units. In the same way there are combinations of various banks to expand their business.

A) Meaning :

A merger is a combination of two or more organisations in which one acquires the assets and liabilities of the other in exchange for shares or cash or both the organisations are dissolved and the assets, liabilities are combined and new stock is issued.

B) Types of Mergers :

Following are the types of mergers :

1) Horizontal Mergers :

Horizontal mergers take place when there is a combination of two or more organisations in the same business, or of organisations engaged in certain aspects of the production or marketing processes. Thus, it is the combination of firms engaged in the same line of activity. For instance, a company making footwear combines with another footwear company, or a retailer of pharmaceuticals combines with another retailer in the same business.

2) Vertical Mergers :

Vertical mergers take place when there is a combination of two or more organisations, not necessarily in the same business, which create complementarity, either in terms of supply of materials i.e. inputs or marketing of goods and services i.e. outputs. Thus, it refers to the combination of firms in successive stages of the same industry. For instance, a footwear company combines with a leather tannery or with a chain of shoe retail stores.

3) Concentric Mergers :

Concentric mergers take place when there is a combination of two or more organisations related to each other either in terms of customer functions, customer groups, or the alternative technologies used. Thus, a footwear company combining with a hosiery firm making socks or another specialty footwear company, or with a leather goods company making purses, handbags and so on.

4.4.2 Acquisitions :

Acquisition is a popular strategic alternative adopted by Indian banking companies. It is a recent trend in banking sector.

A) Meaning :

Acquisitions show the desire of the companies to grow rapidly, compete successfully and neutralise the threats and to avail other benefits. Acquisitions usually are based on the strong motivation of the buyer firm to acquire.

B) Types of Acquisition :

Following are the types of acquisition :

1) Friendly Acquisition :

In case of friendly acquisition, the two companies co-operate with each other and settle matters related to acquisition.

2) Hostile Acquisition :

Sometimes, some groups target a particular company and resort to buying a large number of shares of the target company from the market to grab controlling interest in the company. In India, companies like Shaw Wallace, Dunlop, Father and Platt, Hindustan Dorr Oliver were taken over by Chhabrias in a hostile manner.

4.4.3 Objectives of Mergers and Acquisition :

While the key objective of an M&A always is to grow the organization, they actually take place because of more reasons than one. There can be numerous causes for an M&A to occur. There are several aims that the managers and the company aim for making the union happen. Various objectives of M&A are mentioned below in detail :

1) **Security :**

   There is a security against failure enjoyed by smaller companies when they merge with a huge industry giant. The larger firm has the capacity and financial resources to handle expensive lawsuits and paddle through the market storms. On the other hand, when faced with similar situations, small businesses tend to go bankrupt on their own. The small firms gain the prestige and reputation of a highly respected and well-known industry brand name while large companies gain new talent and ideas. If the M&A is occurring between two moderately-sized companies, they both may consider that combined resources represent a higher security for both.

2) **Scales of Economies :**

   The main objective of M&As is basically to achieve economies of scale, that is, to increase the final output and the firm size as a whole. The cost per item is reduced by spreading the fixed cost over a huge quantity. The efficiency is also increased by specialization of the production process leading to cost advantages. Additionally, by implementing a more effective firm structure, economies of scale are achieved efficiently. Improvement in economies of scale taken place as the firm is able to purchase raw materials in greater quantities, for example, costs can be reduced.

3) **Incentives to Managers :**

   M&As are basically inspired by the goals and personal interests of the company's top management. It is usually guaranteed that the managers enjoy more prestige and power after an M&A. This is also referred to as 'empire building' where the managers begin to favor the size of the firm more than the actual performance. This could be reinforced by the ego of the managers and their intentions for building the biggest company in the industry in terms of size. This is also because the size of the company goes hand-in-hand with the compensation of the managers. Huge companies can afford to give higher salaries and bonuses to their executives and managers. The interests of the managers may not be totally favorable to those of the shareholders.

4) **Diversification :**

   Many times, M&As take place for the purpose of diversification such as offering new products and services or entering into new markets. Furthermore, the risks are also diversified relating to the operations of a company. The shareholders are not always happy with the situation where an M&A occurs with the aim of risk diversification. This is because, in many situations, the shareholders can diversify the risks through investment portfolios easily whereas going through an M&A is a risky and long transaction for this purpose. The conglomerate M&As, market-extension, and product-extension M&As are usually motivated by the objective of diversification.

5) **Tax Benefits :**

When two or more firms merge or during an acquisition, many tax implications arise. Due to an M&A, many tax benefits can be enjoyed by using net operating losses to shield income or taking advantage of existing tax laws. In the case where a loss-making company is acquired by a profit-making firm, the tax burden is reduced by using net operating losses (NOL) of the target firm. Moreover, a company that can upsurge its depreciation charges after an M&A, can save on tax costs and increase in value. The company's surplus funds, unused tax losses, write-up of depreciable assets, and unused debt capacity also create tax benefits.

6) **Eliminating Competition :**

The M&As are done on a large scale for the purpose of eliminating competition in the industry. It is usually done for substantially decreasing competition or for the creation of a monopoly status in the market. This eliminated competition and a solo status can prove very beneficial to the company. They can have the freedom to keep their prices higher and enjoy profits for the business.

7) **Brand Image :**

The mergers that take place on a huge scale create a media giant and demand a higher prestige in the market. Most managers really appreciate the prestige of working and creating for a big company. This can also lead to a rise in their salaries. When two companies merge together, the new brand that is formed enjoys the brand image of both the firms. There is also talent-sharing where the talents of reputed managers are put into this new firm. The good image of the managers also adds to the higher market reputation enjoyed by the resulting company.

8) **Market Share :**

The basic objective behind horizontal M&A is that less number of competitors will increase the prices in a specific market and lead to a rise in market power. This kind of M&A is particularly favorable in saturated markets because internal growth would result in excess in supply and thus decrease in prices. If there are numerous sellers in a competitive type of market, few M&A deals will not affect the pricing power so much. Usually, it is possible for the oligopolistic companies to upsurge their pricing power through M&A. This is however strictly monitored by market authorities and local competition. Whenever an M&A occurs, they gain a higher share in the market which leads to a reduction in competition. Thus, the newly formed company can also raise its prices. There is a proper regulation that takes place by the government for mergers for preventing monopoly to take place. The government wants to avoid a situation where one company owns the complete market for one single product. In such a circumstance, a company can set any price that it likes of the product or service. On the other hand, when there is proper competition, companies are motivated to improve their services and lower their prices to gain consumers, but this can cause a reduction in their profitability too. Since the two firms are in the same industry, collecting their resources may result in a higher market share.

9) Synergy Effect :

When two companies combine together to form a third one, there is a synergy effect achieved as this combination creates an added value. A huge company is considered to bear a low amount of risks, thus, financial synergy is achieved through cheaper access to capital. The main motive is to make the best use of these financial resources for the shareholders and improving overall financial performance. Operational synergy is achieved by combining functions such as distribution and production, or by transfer of knowledge. Managerial synergy is realized when a new management style enters the business from the acquirer to the target company leading to higher efficiency. Management expertise is considered unilateral and transferable. Strategically, the firm is now focused on developing and improving business processes that are closely linked to competitive advantage. A successful M&A results in economies of scale, elimination of certain costs, and access to new technologies.

The occurrence of all these events leads to improvement in the cost structure of a firm. Positive synergies mainly improve the revenue-generating ability of the company leading to product diversification, R&D activities and market expansion. This also increases the wealth of the shareholders.

10) Market Power :

The prime objective of an M&A is to gain a higher share in the market. This helps the company to enjoy the power of monopoly in the industry. Higher prices can be, thus, set by the firm because of this status. Hence, mergers are regulated frequently by the government. However, because the companies operate in several industries, it is debatable whether this specific merger genuinely increases market power.

4.4.4 Characteristics of Mergers and Acquisition :

The consolidation of companies is called Mergers and Acquisitions (M&A). If we differentiate both the terms, mergers refer to the combination of two companies to form one, while acquisitions are one company taking over the other company. One of the major aspects of the corporate finance world is M&A. Undoubtedly, it is the fastest way to grow small businesses. Value creation is the prime feature of M&As as two separate companies come together into an individual stand due to this reason. Along with the benefits, there are certain risks involved in these unions too which cannot be ignored. During an M&A process, the prime aspects and characteristics are given as follows:

1) **Communication :**

   During any Merger or Acquisition (M&A), communication is the key as these types of events are very crucial in nature. This is not only applicable to communication between the two executives or owners of both the companies in question, but also the subordinates and employees. If proper and adequate information is not passed on to the employees, they are going to look for other jobs because they might lack security here. During such a critical process, low employee retention can really be harmful to the company.

2) **Growth and Development :**

   The main purpose of M&As is usually the growth and development of the business. Any business that wants to grow has basically two options, either acquire a company or just star up some new project. Only the rise in production volume is not growth. Growth can be geographically, demographically, and in products too. New goods and services can be brought up by the business which is also called product/service expansion. Also, new locations and countries can be targeted for expansion. Many M&As take place between companies of different countries so that the firms reach new areas for conducting business globally. New audiences are also targeted for the purpose of business development. Businesses may be able to add to their distribution network or expand its geographic service area by expanding geographically.

3) **Transparency :**

   Transparency is absolutely necessary throughout the M&A process. Right from the initial discussion to the commencement of the new firm and after that too, there must be open discussion and honest communication between the parties. Everything must be made clear prior to avoid any confusion in the future. A non-disclosure agreement is also signed most of the time for risking the limit of somebody withholding information. This is done among all the parties who have direct involvement in this event. The information must be disclosed very carefully regarding legal situations, business finances, and anything other than that which could have an impact on the purchase. This is legally required in many cases.

4) **Defined Goals :**

   Well-defined goals are a very important pre-requisite during the accomplishment of mergers and acquisitions. When a company is purchasing another business, a predesigned goal or objective is necessary because the vision of the acquisition should be well thought-after. When a successful Merger and Acquisition (M&A) takes place, the territories are expanded, sales are boosted, patents are acquired and an all-new market is entered. The aims of the business are identified at an early stage so that the processes can be started on the right foot.

5) **Discounted Cash Flow (DCF) :**

A prime valuation tool in M&A is a discounted cash flow analysis that determines the current value of the company. This is calculated on the basis of forecasted future cash flows. The estimated free cash flows are discounted in comparison to the present value using the weighted average costs of capital (WACC) of the company. This value is difficult to get, but with the help of a few tools, this valuation method can work easily.

6) **Replacement Cost :**

Considering various cases, acquisition is many times based on the cost of replacement of the target company. It takes a long period of time for assembling good management, purchase of right equipment and acquiring a property. This method is used to establish a certain price but does not make sense in a service industry where the prime assets are ideas and people. Costs can be reduced by eliminating staffing redundancies.

7) **Multiple Bidders :**

The most profitable deal for sellers normally occurs when there are several potential bidders. Sellers can obtain better deal terms, a higher price, or both by leveraging the competitive situation. The selling company can go into a significant disadvantage if they negotiate with just one single bidder. This is mainly when the selling company agrees on signing an exclusivity agreement that limits its ability to speak to other potential buyers for a specific period of time.

Most of the time, the sellers try to set up a competitive bidding process or an auction to avoid being restricted by exclusive demands. Every bidder can be played off against another for arriving at a favorable deal. There can be cases where there is only one serious potential bidder but the perception where there are numerous parties interested really helps in the negotiations.

▶ 4.5 Franchising :

Franchise is a kind of authorisation granted to an individual or corporation by a franchisor to sell its goods or services in a defined way. In simple words, franchise is nothing but a license allowing a person or company to use or sell specific products in certain areas as per agreement.

4.5.1 Meaning :

Franchising is a long-term co-operative relationship between two entities a franchisor and one or more franchisees that is based on an agreement in which the franchisor provides a licensed privilege to the franchisee to do business. The franchisor grants the franchisee the right to use a developed concept, including trademarks and brand names, production, service and marketing methods and the entire business operation model, for a fee. The franchisee then provides the time, capital, and desire to utilise the brand and services provided by the franchisor to build a thriving business. The product method or service being marketed is usually identified by the franchisor's brand name, and the holder of the privilege (franchisee) is often given exclusive access to a defined geographical area for a defined period of time, all of which is defined in the Franchise Agreement.

4.5.2 Definition :

Definition of franchising is as follows :

1) **The International Franchise Association :**

   "A contractual relationship between the franchisor and the franchisee in which the franchisor offers or is obliged to maintain a continuing interest in the business of the franchisee in such areas as know-how and training; wherein the franchisee operates under a common trade name, format or procedure owned by or controlled by the franchisor, and in which the franchisee has made or will make a substantial capital investment in his business from his own resources."

4.5.3 Characteristics of Franchising :

Franchises may be less risky than independent businesses, but there are still varying degrees of success and profitability associated with being a franchisee. Some franchises are far more profitable than others. Here are some characteristics associated with highly profitable franchises:

1) **Provides Well Established Profitable Business :**

   A franchise is a readymade and well-established business. As franchise business is already set up by the franchisor, the initial investment required by the franchisee to enter and establish is relatively low. As the goodwill and reputation is already set up in other countries, franchisor does not require more efforts to enter in new markets. He is easily accepted in the new markets. The franchisor allows the franchisee to use his brand name, trademark, and service mark and management skills for developing and expanding franchise business.

2) **Pre-opening Benefits :**

   The cost of entrance into a franchise system includes a franchise fee, which is often cited as a disadvantage. However, the franchisee benefits from the franchisor's having tested operating systems, specialised training for management and staff, operations manuals, marketing and advertising programs, store design, the reduced cost of equipment, and the other necessary support required to successfully launch their business. The Franchisee does not have to bother about any setting up issues.

3) Overall Competitive Benefits :

People are accustomed to a certain level of quality and consistency from branded locations. A branded location is a business that the public thinks of as a chain because each location has the same name, decor, products, services, menu items, and so on. The customer experience is the same regardless of the location. Regardless of where they are, consumers believe they understand the level of quality they will receive when they shop at a branded location. It is because of this perception about branded chains; new franchisees often have an established customer base on the day they open. Branding enables franchises to compete with the well-established, independent operators and even against other franchised and non-franchised chains. E.g. McDonald's, KFC, Big-Bazaar.

4) Ongoing Benefits :

Franchisees benefit from the field-consulting assistance most franchisors provide. Franchisees enjoy the purchasing power that comes from joining with others, which often results in a reduced cost of goods. They benefit from professionally designed point-of-sale marketing material, advertising, grand-opening programs, and other marketing materials that independents could never afford. Franchise systems can also afford to modernise through ongoing research and development and by test marketing new products and operating systems.

4.5.4 Advantages of Franchising :

Following are the advantages of franchising :

1) Higher success Rate :

When entrepreneurs buy a franchise, they buy an established concept that has been successful. Franchisees stand a much better chance of success than people who start independent businesses.

Today, Raymonds, being the world's largest integrated producers of suiting fabrics provides franchise opportunities. An entrepreneur by becoming a franchisee of Raymonds will be able to sell the suiting fabrics at ease due to the well established name.

2) Assistance :

When entrepreneurs buy a franchise; they get all the equipment, supplies and instruction or training needed to start the business.

3) Cost Reduction :

Franchisor can afford to buy in bulk and pass the savings to franchisees. Inventory and supplies will cost less than running an independent company. For example, running a courier company on own could be a difficult task. But by being a franchisee of Overnite Express, the franchisee can save money.

4) **Star Power :**

Many well-known franchises have national brand-name recognition. Buying a franchise can be like buying a business with built-in customers. For example, buying a franchise of Aptech will help to attract customers easily.

5) **Profits :**

A franchise business can be immensely profitable. The probability for a small business to succeed is high as they have the backup and support of well-established big business enterprises.

6) **Marketing Assistance :**

When a business is associated with a franchisor then the big-business themselves help in corporate marketing of the goods of the small industry or business they are providing support for.

7) **Staff Training :**

The franchisor provides all the necessary training to the franchisee or small business staff and provides additional resources and decision-making capabilities to a small business.

4.5.5 Disadvantages/Limitations of Franchising :

Following re the disadvantages / limitation of franchising :

1) **Control :**

Some franchisors exert a great degree of control. No decision can be taken by the franchisees without consulting the franchisor.

2) **Ongoing Costs :**

Besides the original franchise fee, royalties, a percentage of franchise's business revenue, will have to be paid to the franchisor each month.

3) **Lack of Support :**

All franchisors do not offer the same degree of assistance in starting a business and operating it successfully. Assistance is provided only at the time of starting the business.

4) **Expensive :**

Buying a well-known franchise is very expensive. Entrepreneurs must have the ability to arrange the necessary finance.

5) **Time consuming :**

Lot of time is required while selecting a franchise. A complete and thorough research is required to select the right franchise and to determine whether it would work for the business or not.

6) **Misunderstanding :**

Franchise is a complex procedure and disputes may arise between the franchisee and franchisor.

▶ 4.6 Public Private Partnership :

A Public-private partnership (PPP) is often defined as a long-term contract between a private party and a government agency for providing a public asset or service, in which the private party bears significant risk and management responsibility (World Bank, 2012). It relies on the recognition that public and private sectors each have certain advantages relative to other in performing specific tasks. The responsibilities of the private sector could entail finance, design, construction, operation, management and maintenance of the project. The PPP model is well-established for the construction of economic and social infrastructure and is now used in more than half of the world's countries. The model is well-established for the construction of economic infrastructure such as roads, bridges and public transport systems but it is also used for social infrastructure such as schools, prisons, and hospital.

4.6.1 Meaning :

A public–private partnership (PPP, 3P, or P3) is a cooperative arrangement between two or more public and private sectors, typically of a long-term nature. In other words, it involves government(s) and business (es) that work together to complete a project and/or to provide services to the population. They are an example of multi stakeholder governance which is a key target of United Nations Sustainable Development Goal 17. Public–private partnerships have been implemented in multiple countries, are primarily used for infrastructure projects, such as the building and equipping of schools, hospitals, transport systems, and water and sewerage systems.

4.6.2 Features of Public-Private Partnership :

To understand the PPP concept, we must know its fundamental characteristics. Some of these are discussed in detail below :

1) **Service-Oriented :**

   The PPP approach deals with the facilitation of long-term public services. It includes roads for transportation, dams for electricity and water supply and street lights for lighting.

2) **Whole Life Costing :**

   In the PPP model, the project's total cost is computed at once for its entire life span. Thus, taking into consideration the initial capital expenditure, repair and maintenance expenses, modification expense and the eventual disposition cost.

3) **Innovation :**

   With the involvement of the private firms, the PPP approach also initiates the implications of creativity and new technology to the infrastructure projects.

4) **Participants :**

   The two parties involved in the public-private alliance are; the government and the respective private company.

5) **Risk Allocation :**
Infrastructure projects involve high risk; thus, PPP helps the government to transfer this risk to private firms.

6) **Long-term Relationship :**
These projects are usually for years; therefore, the government authority and the private entity remains associated for an extended period.

7) **Resource Sharing :**
The capital, financial, design and other resources required, are shared between the government and the firm for successful project accomplished.

4.6.3 Types of Public Private Partnership :

Following are the types of public private partnership :

1) **Build-Operate-Transfer (BOT) :**
The toll road construction projects are illustrated under this conventional model. The private company constructs the road, collect toll or revenue (for the contract period) and then pass its possession to the government.

2) **Build-Own-Operate (BOO) :**
It is though very similar to the BOT model; here, the possession of the facility remains with the private entity itself.

3) **Build-Own-Operate-Transfer (BOOT) :**
To recover the cost of construction and incur gains, the private firm, after development, keeps the possession of the facility up to the contract period. After which it passes on the ownership to the public sector.

4) **Build-Lease-Operate-Transfer (BLOT) :**
The private company uses a leased public property to develop a facility. It functions on this property for the lease period to recover cost and earn revenue. Later as the lease expires, the land is handed over, back to the government.

5) **Design-Build (DB) :**
This is the basic form of P3 where the private company layouts and constructs the facility as per the government requirements, after complete risk assessment. In return, it takes a fixed amount as its charges.

6) **Design-Build-Finance (DBF) :**
The private sector firm undertakes a project to design the layout, build the facility and meet the capital cost involved in such designing and construction.

7) **Design-Build-Finance-Operate (DBFO) :**
In the DBFO model, the private company is responsible for planning the project layout, facility construction, arranging the required capital and operating it till the grant period. The facility operations revenue meets the cost incurred and generates profit to the company.

8) **Design-Build-Finance-Maintain (DBFM) :**

This model can also be termed as a management contract. Here, the public sector entity remains associated with the project from the beginning to the end. The process starts right from designing of the layout, to construction, funding and lifetime maintenance of the facility. The firm either charges a fixed sum or shares profit; also, it is involved in the project's managerial decision making.

9) **Design-Build-Finance-Maintain-Operate (DBFMO) :**

It is an extended version of DBFO. Here, the private firm prepares the blueprint, builds up the facility, invest the required sum and carry out the operations to generate revenue. Since the company undertakes the project for a long-term, it has to take care of the maintenance work too.

10) **Design-Construct-Maintain-Finance (DCMF) :**

In the DCMF model, the private entity understands the government specifications and accordingly designs, develops, upkeeps and invest in a facility. This facility is then leased out to the government body itself.

11) **Operation and Maintenance(O&M) :**

This model involves assigning of a sub-contract to the private companies for running and up keeping a facility.

The firms which undertake such projects are experts in maintenance work. Also, the possession of the facility remains with the government body. The revenue for private entities is commonly generated through a performance-based fee. In some cases, the companies charge a lump sum and fixed price for their services.

4.6.4 Advantages of Public-Private Partnership (PPP) :

The PPP approach is highly beneficial for the government, the country, the economy, the private organizations and the public. Given below are some of the prominent pros of this concept :

1) **Early Completion Bonus :**

To improve efficiency, the private companies are motivated through bonus if they complete the project before time.

2) **Cut Downs Tax :**

The cost-efficient infrastructure project helps the government to save funds and thus, provides for a reduction in the tax rates.

3) **Project Completion Efficiency :**

When the standard time for completing a project is estimated, its execution and fulfillment become more competent.

4) **Project Feasibility :**

As the project's risk involvement and practical implementation are well-analyzed, the chances of failure reduces remarkably.

5) **Superior Quality Standards :**
PPP approach initiates benchmarking for the desired quality of the project and ensuring the same during the project's life cycle.

6) **Excellent Infrastructure Solutions :**
This has been possible since, the proficient private companies work in collaboration with the government, where each of them contributes their best.

7) **Better Return on Investment :**
The ROI of the P3 infrastructure projects might be reasonably high in the long run. The reason being it has been monitored and accomplished by both parties together.

8) **Transfer of Risk :**
The government hands over the associated risk along with the project to the private firms who have relevant experience and knowledge in the area.

9) **Reduces Budget Deficits :**
In the PPP approach, the private companies determine the cost and perform the capital budgeting to avoid any shortage of funds in future.

10) **Ensures Efficient Government Investment :**
Since P3 initially let the private companies invest their funds in the infrastructure projects, the government can utilize its capital for socio-economic welfare.

4.6.5 Disadvantages of Public-Private Partnership (PPP) :

On the one hand, it helps to improve the infrastructure conditions in a country. Whereas, on the other hand, it has the following limitations :

1) **Involves Risk for Private Firms :**
The public-private partnership provides for the transfer of risk to the private entities, overburdening them with the responsibility of failure.

2) **Varying Profitability :**
The complexity, competition level, associated risk, nature, size and impact of the project determines its profitability.

3) **Raise Government Expenses :**
Due to the project's high-risk involvement, the companies usually demand huge compensation, leading to a hike in government expenses.

4) **May not be Cost-Efficient :**
At times, the government lacks sufficient knowledge of the project cost. When the private company holds the complete cost information; the public sector may be misled.

5) **Dependency on Private Sector :**
The most significant limitation of the PPP approach is that the government majorly relies on the private sector for project undertaking and accomplishment.

Objective Type Questions

Q. I. Multiple Choice Questions :

1) Which of the following is NOT a strategic alliance?

a) Joint marketing campaign
b) Cooperative product development
c) Joint venture
d) Merger

2) What is the most frequent internal motive for a strategic alliance?

a) Resource need
b) Risk limitation
c) Cost minimization
d) Current poor performance

3) An acquisition is the same thing as:

a) a merger
b) an amalgamation
c) a takeover
d) a spin-off

4) The ways in which mergers and acquisitions (M&As) occur do not include:

a) vertical integration
b) diversification
c) horizontal integration
d) conglomerate takeover

5) The 'good' reasons for M&As do not include ------------.

a) stopping a competitor merging or taking over
b) supporting value-added growth
c) complementing business strategies
d) increasing earnings per share

6) Justifications for M&As do not include ------------.

a) to gain economies of scale
b) to increase risk
c) to enter new markets
d) to achieve synergy

7) Financial motives for M&As do not relate to ------------.

a) value added tax
b) corporation tax
c) unemployed tax shields
d) earnings per share

8) Managerial motives for M&As do not relate to ------------.

a) power
b) job security
c) emoluments
d) dividends

9) When a company enters into a legal arrangement to allow its product, services, or business-format to be used by others for a fee it is called ------------.

a) franchisee
b) franchising
c) franchisor
d) unrealistic

10) A company or individual who pays for the legal right to use the product, service, or format of another is called a ------------.

a) franchisee
b) franchisor
c) franchising
d) lunatic

11) Business-format franchising ------------.

a) accounts for nearly 75 percent of all franchised outlets in the United States

b) has revolutionized the retailing of automobiles

c) was developed by General Motors

d) all of the above

12) Among the different forms of franchising are ------------.

a) business-format franchising

b) product franchising

c) manufacturing franchising

d) all of the above

13) The main characteristic of PPP is ------------.

a) long term (sometimes up to 30 years) service provisions

b) The transfer of risks to the private sector

c) different forms of long-term contracts drawn up between legal entities and public authorities

d) All of the above

14) What is the ingredient common to all types of PPP?

a) The public sector transfers the overall responsibility to provide the public service

b) value for money will be the basic criterion for the public sector

c) No balanced sharing of the risks and gains between the public sector and private sector

d) none of the above

15) The common characteristic of Institutional PPPs and contractual PPPs is ------------.

a) The operation of a facility is contracted out to another private party

b) The users pay for the facility availed and such charges accrue to the private sector partner

c) The public sector usually designs, constructs and operate PPP

d) none of the above

16) The main difference between PPP and privatization is ------------.

a) There is no permanent transfer of ownership of assets to private partner

b) The responsibility and accountability to deliver the goods and services remains with the state/public sector

c) Besides the transfer of ownership to the private sector, the accountability is also shifted to the purchaser

d) none of the above

17) What distinguishes each type of PPP model from one another is ------------.

a) the degree of risk and responsibility borne by the private sector partner

b) the degree of risk and responsibility borne by the public sector

c) The private sector partner will bring in most of the investment requirements

d) none of the above

Ans : **1)** d, **2)** a, **3)** c, **4)** b, **5)** d, **6)** b, **7)** a, **8)** d, **9)** b, **10)** a, **11)** a, **12)** d, **13)** d, **14)** b, **15)** b, **16)** b, **17)** a.

Q. II. State the following statement are true or false :

1) If management is primarily concerned with the long-term value of a merger, it is more likely to use the earnings-per-share approach to analyzing the merger's benefits.

2) The acquisition of a coal mining business by a steel manufacturing company is an example of a vertical merger.

3) Most M&A transactions in the United States are hostile or unfriendly takeover attempts.

4) Because of the mark-up charges by the franchiser, the cost of materials and supplies are always higher than what the franchisee would pay on the open market.

5) The business plan for "buying a franchise" includes all five sections of the basic "start-up" business plan.

6) The word "franchise" refers to a set of rights for operating a business.

7) Because of the government's interest in protecting parties involved in franchising, the prospective franchisee must notify the franchiser within two weeks after receiving the franchise agreement or lose out on the deal.

8) Public-private partnerships involve collaboration between a government agency and private-sector companies that can be used to finance, build, and operate projects, such as public transportation networks, parks, and convention centers.

Ans : **1)** True, **2)** True, **3)** False, **4)** False, **5)** True, **6)** True, **7)** False, **8)** True.

Review Questions

Q. 1. What is mean by Merger and Acquisition? Explain the Characteristic of Mergers and Acquisition.

Q. 2. Explain the Objectives of Mergers and Acquisition.

Q. 3. What do you mean by Franchising? Explain the Characteristics of Franchising.

Q. 4. Discuss the Advantages and Disadvantages of Franchising.

Q. 5. What do you mean by Outsourcing? Explain the Characteristics of Outsourcing.

Q. 6. Discuss in detail about the Advantages and Disadvantages of Outsourcing.

Q. 7. What do you mean by Public Private Partnership? Explain the Types of Public Private Partnership.

Q. 8. Explain the Features of Public Private Partnership.

Q. 9. Discuss in detail about the Advantages and Disadvantages of Public Private Partnership.

Q. 10. Explain the Concept of Business Engineering. Discuss the Importance of Business Engineering.

Q. 11. Write Short Notes on Following:

a) Types of Mergers.

b) Types of Acquisition.

c) Types of Public Private Partnership.

d) Advantages of Outsourcing.

e) Disadvantages of Outsourcing.

f) Advantages of Public Private Partnership.

g) Disadvantages of Public Private Partnership.

❋❋❋❋